LIFE IS TOO SHORT TO SMOKE BAD CIGARS

This Book Belongs to:

_____

_____

_____

@United Publishing. All rights reserved.
No part of this publication may be reproduced in any form
without the permission of the publisher.

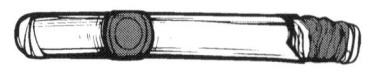

Cigar Tasting Journal

	NAME				
	BRAND			TYPE	
	WRAPPER			FILLER	
	ORIGIN			SAMPLED	

Label

Flavor Meter

	BODY	VERY MILD	MILD	MEDIUM	MED-FULL	FULL
	FLAVOR	VERY MILD	MILD	MEDIUM	MED-FULL	FULL
	STRENGTH	VERY MILD	MILD	MEDIUM	MED-FULL	FULL

Notes

Flavor Wheel

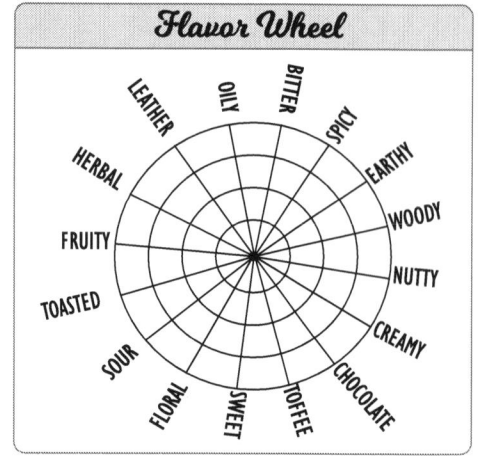

Appearance	Value For Money	Flavor
★☆☆☆☆	★☆☆☆☆	★☆☆☆☆

Would you try again?	Overall Rating
☐ YES ☐ NO	★☆☆☆☆

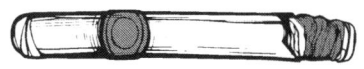

Cigar Tasting Journal

	NAME				
	BRAND			TYPE	
	WRAPPER			FILLER	
	ORIGIN			SAMPLED	

Label

CIGAR LABEL HERE

Flavor Meter

BODY	VERY MILD	MILD	MEDIUM	MED-FULL	FULL
FLAVOR	VERY MILD	MILD	MEDIUM	MED-FULL	FULL
STRENGTH	VERY MILD	MILD	MEDIUM	MED-FULL	FULL

Notes

Flavor Wheel

Appearance	Value For Money	Flavor
★☆☆☆☆	★☆☆☆☆	★☆☆☆☆

Would you try again?		Overall Rating
☐ YES	☐ NO	★☆☆☆☆

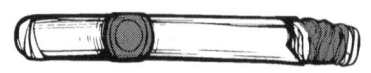

Cigar Tasting Journal

NAME			
BRAND		TYPE	
WRAPPER		FILLER	
ORIGIN		SAMPLED	

Label

Flavor Meter

	VERY MILD	MILD	MEDIUM	MED-FULL	FULL
BODY					
FLAVOR					
STRENGTH					

Notes

Flavor Wheel

Appearance	Value For Money	Flavor
★☆☆☆☆	★☆☆☆☆	★☆☆☆☆

Would you try again?	Overall Rating
☐ YES ☐ NO	★☆☆☆☆

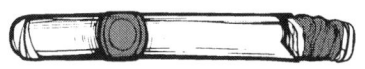

Cigar Tasting Journal

	NAME			TYPE	
	BRAND			FILLER	
	WRAPPER				
	ORIGIN			SAMPLED	

Label

CIGAR LABEL HERE

Flavor Meter

		VERY MILD	MILD	MEDIUM	MED-FULL	FULL
	BODY					
	FLAVOR					
	STRENGTH					

Notes

Flavor Wheel

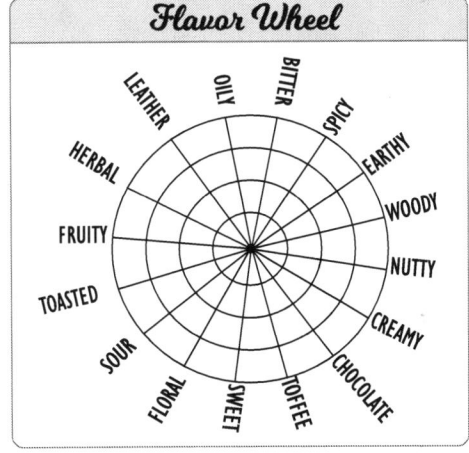

Appearance	Value For Money	Flavor
★☆☆☆☆	★☆☆☆☆	★☆☆☆☆

Would you try again?		Overall Rating
☐ YES	☐ NO	★☆☆☆☆

Cigar Tasting Journal

NAME			
BRAND		TYPE	
WRAPPER		FILLER	
ORIGIN		SAMPLED	

Label

Flavor Meter

	VERY MILD	MILD	MEDIUM	MED-FULL	FULL
BODY					
FLAVOR					
STRENGTH					

Notes

Flavor Wheel

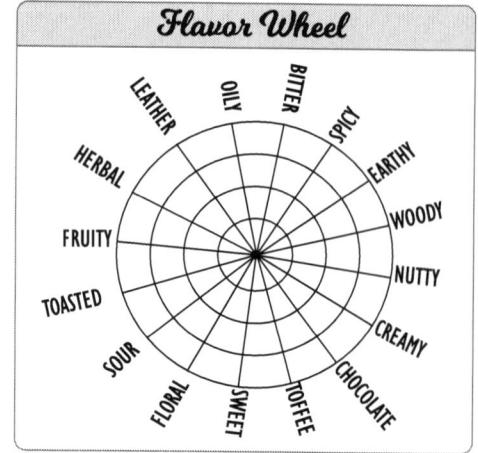

Appearance	Value For Money	Flavor
★☆☆☆☆	★☆☆☆☆	★☆☆☆☆

Would you try again?		Overall Rating
☐ YES	☐ NO	★☆☆☆☆

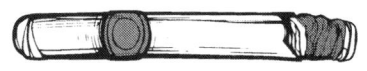

Cigar Tasting Journal

NAME			
BRAND		TYPE	
WRAPPER		FILLER	
ORIGIN		SAMPLED	

Label

CIGAR LABEL HERE

Flavor Meter

	VERY MILD	MILD	MEDIUM	MED-FULL	FULL
BODY					
FLAVOR					
STRENGTH					

Notes

Flavor Wheel

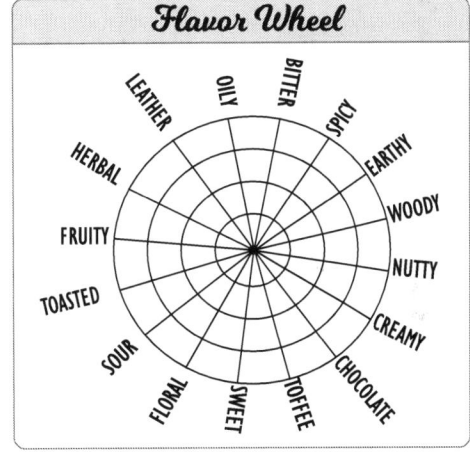

Appearance	Value For Money	Flavor
★☆☆☆☆	★☆☆☆☆	★☆☆☆☆

Would you try again?	Overall Rating
☐ YES ☐ NO	★☆☆☆☆

Cigar Tasting Journal

	NAME				
	BRAND			TYPE	
	WRAPPER			FILLER	
	ORIGIN			SAMPLED	

Label

Flavor Meter

BODY	VERY MILD	MILD	MEDIUM	MED-FULL	FULL
FLAVOR	VERY MILD	MILD	MEDIUM	MED-FULL	FULL
STRENGTH	VERY MILD	MILD	MEDIUM	MED-FULL	FULL

Notes

Flavor Wheel

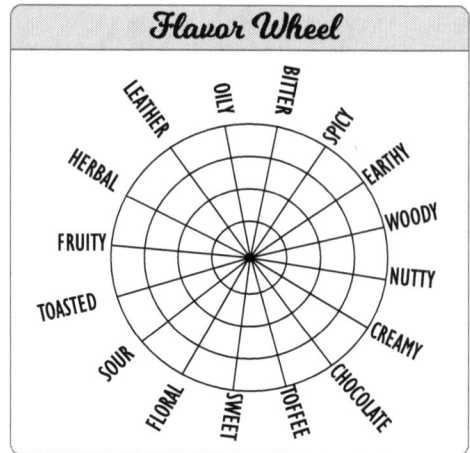

Appearance	Value For Money	Flavor
★☆☆☆☆	★☆☆☆☆	★☆☆☆☆

Would you try again?		Overall Rating
☐ YES	☐ NO	★☆☆☆☆

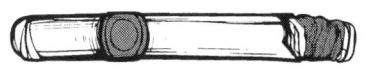

Cigar Tasting Journal

NAME				
BRAND		TYPE		
WRAPPER		FILLER		
ORIGIN		SAMPLED		

Label

Flavor Meter

	VERY MILD	MILD	MEDIUM	MED-FULL	FULL
BODY					
FLAVOR					
STRENGTH					

Notes

Flavor Wheel

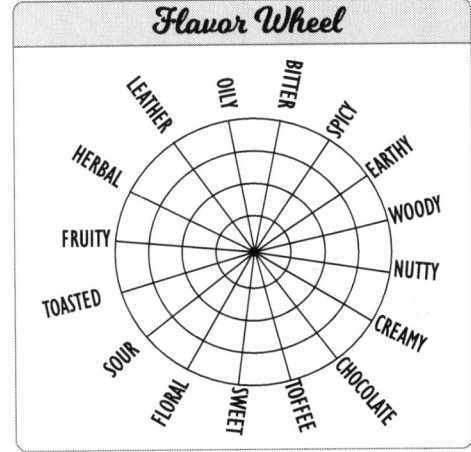

Appearance	Value For Money	Flavor
★☆☆☆☆	★☆☆☆☆	★☆☆☆☆

Would you try again?		Overall Rating
☐ YES	☐ NO	★☆☆☆☆

Cigar Tasting Journal

NAME			
BRAND		TYPE	
WRAPPER		FILLER	
ORIGIN		SAMPLED	

Label

Flavor Meter

	VERY MILD	MILD	MEDIUM	MED-FULL	FULL
BODY					
FLAVOR					
STRENGTH					

Notes

Flavor Wheel

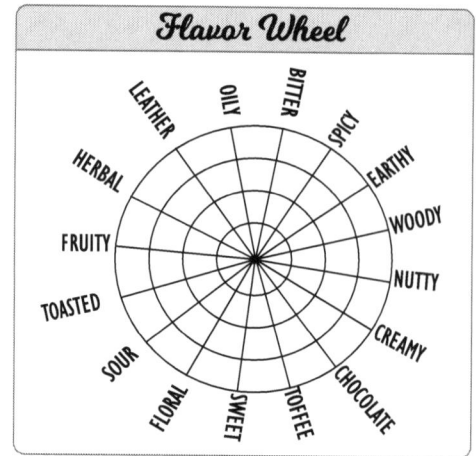

Appearance	Value For Money	Flavor
☆☆☆☆☆	☆☆☆☆☆	☆☆☆☆☆

Would you try again?		Overall Rating
☐ YES	☐ NO	☆☆☆☆☆

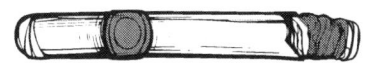

Cigar Tasting Journal

	NAME			TYPE	
	BRAND			FILLER	
	WRAPPER			SAMPLED	
	ORIGIN				

Label

CIGAR LABEL HERE

Flavor Meter

	BODY	VERY MILD	MILD	MEDIUM	MED-FULL	FULL
	FLAVOR	VERY MILD	MILD	MEDIUM	MED-FULL	FULL
	STRENGTH	VERY MILD	MILD	MEDIUM	MED-FULL	FULL

Notes

Flavor Wheel

Appearance	Value For Money	Flavor
★☆☆☆☆	★☆☆☆☆	★☆☆☆☆

Would you try again?		Overall Rating
☐ YES	☐ NO	★☆☆☆☆

Cigar Tasting Journal

	NAME				
	BRAND			TYPE	
	WRAPPER			FILLER	
	ORIGIN			SAMPLED	

Label

Flavor Meter

BODY		VERY MILD	MILD	MEDIUM	MED-FULL	FULL
FLAVOR		VERY MILD	MILD	MEDIUM	MED-FULL	FULL
STRENGTH		VERY MILD	MILD	MEDIUM	MED-FULL	FULL

Notes

Flavor Wheel

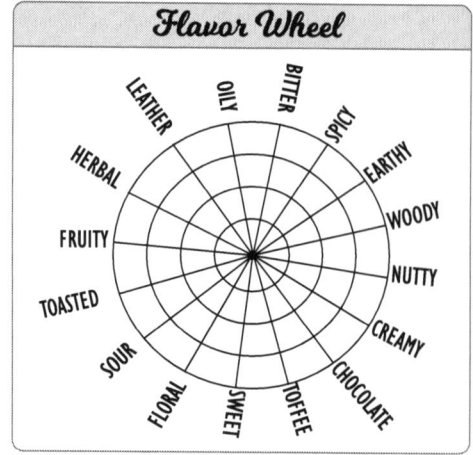

Appearance	Value For Money	Flavor
★☆☆☆☆	★☆☆☆☆	★☆☆☆☆

Would you try again?		Overall Rating
☐ YES	☐ NO	★☆☆☆☆

Cigar Tasting Journal

	NAME				
	BRAND			TYPE	
	WRAPPER			FILLER	
	ORIGIN			SAMPLED	

Label

CIGAR LABEL HERE

Flavor Meter

		VERY MILD	MILD	MEDIUM	MED-FULL	FULL
	BODY					
	FLAVOR					
	STRENGTH					

Notes

Flavor Wheel

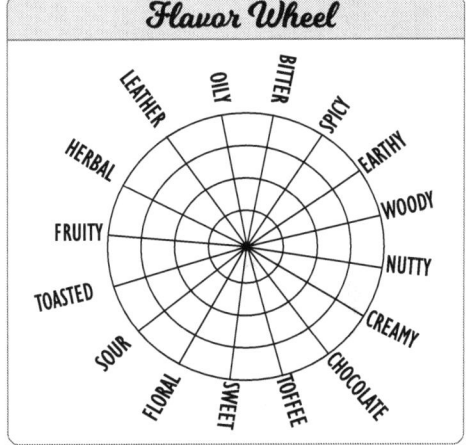

Appearance	Value For Money	Flavor
★☆☆☆☆	★☆☆☆☆	★☆☆☆☆

Would you try again?		Overall Rating
☐ YES	☐ NO	★☆☆☆☆

Cigar Tasting Journal

	NAME				
	BRAND			TYPE	
	WRAPPER			FILLER	
	ORIGIN			SAMPLED	

Label

CIGAR LABEL HERE

Flavor Meter

	BODY	VERY MILD	MILD	MEDIUM	MED-FULL	FULL
	FLAVOR	VERY MILD	MILD	MEDIUM	MED-FULL	FULL
	STRENGTH	VERY MILD	MILD	MEDIUM	MED-FULL	FULL

Notes

Flavor Wheel

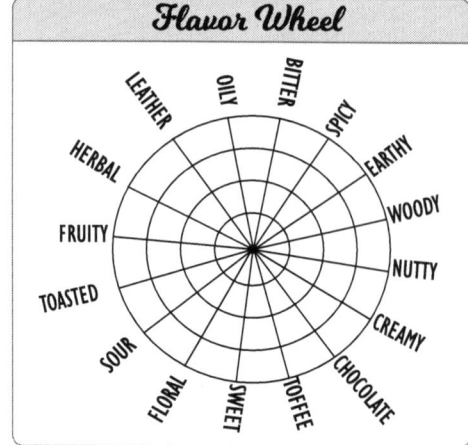

Appearance	Value For Money	Flavor
★☆☆☆☆	★☆☆☆☆	★☆☆☆☆

Would you try again?		Overall Rating
☐ YES	☐ NO	★☆☆☆☆

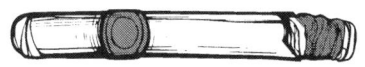

Cigar Tasting Journal

NAME				
BRAND		TYPE		
WRAPPER		FILLER		
ORIGIN		SAMPLED		

Label

CIGAR LABEL HERE

Flavor Meter

	VERY MILD	MILD	MEDIUM	MED-FULL	FULL
BODY					
FLAVOR					
STRENGTH					

Notes

Flavor Wheel

Appearance	Value For Money	Flavor
★☆☆☆☆	★☆☆☆☆	★☆☆☆☆

Would you try again?		Overall Rating
☐ YES	☐ NO	★☆☆☆☆

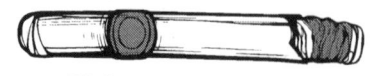

Cigar Tasting Journal

	NAME			TYPE	
	BRAND			FILLER	
	WRAPPER			SAMPLED	
	ORIGIN				

Label

Flavor Meter

		VERY MILD	MILD	MEDIUM	MED-FULL	FULL
	BODY	VERY MILD	MILD	MEDIUM	MED-FULL	FULL
	FLAVOR	VERY MILD	MILD	MEDIUM	MED-FULL	FULL
	STRENGTH	VERY MILD	MILD	MEDIUM	MED-FULL	FULL

Notes

Flavor Wheel

Appearance	Value For Money	Flavor
★☆☆☆☆	★☆☆☆☆	★☆☆☆☆

Would you try again?		Overall Rating
☐ YES	☐ NO	★☆☆☆☆

Cigar Tasting Journal

NAME				
BRAND		TYPE		
WRAPPER		FILLER		
ORIGIN		SAMPLED		

Label

CIGAR LABEL HERE

Flavor Meter

	VERY MILD	MILD	MEDIUM	MED-FULL	FULL
BODY					
FLAVOR					
STRENGTH					

Notes

Flavor Wheel

Flavors: BITTER, OILY, LEATHER, HERBAL, FRUITY, TOASTED, SOUR, FLORAL, SWEET, TOFFEE, CHOCOLATE, CREAMY, NUTTY, WOODY, EARTHY, SPICY

Appearance	Value For Money	Flavor
★☆☆☆☆	★☆☆☆☆	★☆☆☆☆

Would you try again?		Overall Rating
☐ YES	☐ NO	★☆☆☆☆

Cigar Tasting Journal

	NAME			TYPE	
	BRAND			FILLER	
	WRAPPER			SAMPLED	
	ORIGIN				

Label

Flavor Meter

		VERY MILD	MILD	MEDIUM	MED-FULL	FULL
	BODY					
	FLAVOR					
	STRENGTH					

Notes

Flavor Wheel

Appearance	Value For Money	Flavor
★☆☆☆☆	★☆☆☆☆	★☆☆☆☆

Would you try again?		Overall Rating
☐ YES	☐ NO	★☆☆☆☆

Cigar Tasting Journal

NAME		TYPE		
BRAND		FILLER		
WRAPPER		SAMPLED		
ORIGIN				

Label

CIGAR LABEL HERE

Flavor Meter

	VERY MILD	MILD	MEDIUM	MED-FULL	FULL
BODY					
FLAVOR					
STRENGTH					

Notes

Flavor Wheel

LEATHER, OILY, BITTER, SPICY, EARTHY, WOODY, NUTTY, CREAMY, CHOCOLATE, TOFFEE, SWEET, FLORAL, SOUR, TOASTED, FRUITY, HERBAL

Appearance	Value For Money	Flavor
★☆☆☆☆	★☆☆☆☆	★☆☆☆☆

Would you try again?	Overall Rating
☐ YES ☐ NO	★☆☆☆☆

Cigar Tasting Journal

NAME			
BRAND		TYPE	
WRAPPER		FILLER	
ORIGIN		SAMPLED	

Label

Flavor Meter

	VERY MILD	MILD	MEDIUM	MED-FULL	FULL
BODY					
FLAVOR					
STRENGTH					

Notes

Flavor Wheel

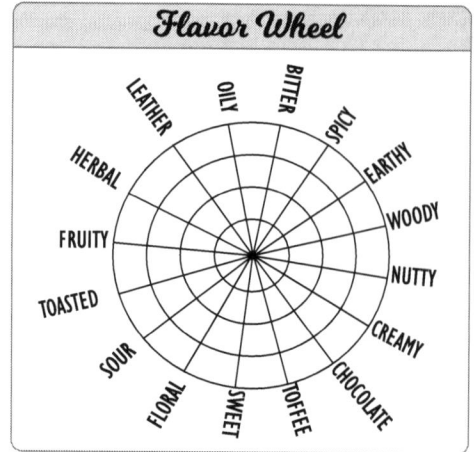

Flavors: LEATHER, OILY, BITTER, SPICY, EARTHY, WOODY, NUTTY, CREAMY, CHOCOLATE, TOFFEE, SWEET, FLORAL, SOUR, TOASTED, FRUITY, HERBAL

Appearance	Value For Money	Flavor
☆☆☆☆☆	☆☆☆☆☆	☆☆☆☆☆

Would you try again?		Overall Rating
☐ YES	☐ NO	☆☆☆☆☆

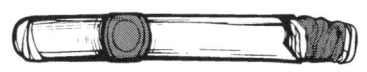

Cigar Tasting Journal

	NAME				
	BRAND			TYPE	
	WRAPPER			FILLER	
	ORIGIN			SAMPLED	

Label

CIGAR LABEL HERE

Flavor Meter

		VERY MILD	MILD	MEDIUM	MED-FULL	FULL
	BODY					
	FLAVOR					
	STRENGTH					

Notes

Flavor Wheel

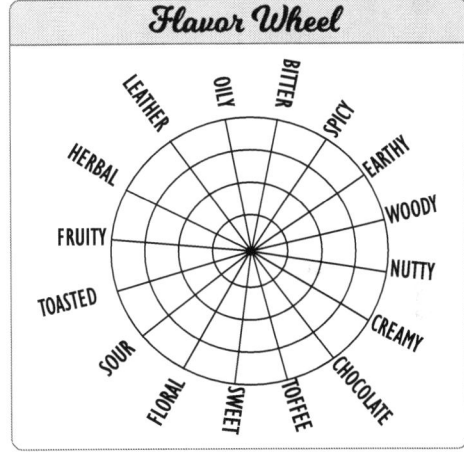

BITTER, SPICY, EARTHY, WOODY, NUTTY, CREAMY, CHOCOLATE, TOFFEE, SWEET, FLORAL, SOUR, TOASTED, FRUITY, HERBAL, LEATHER, OILY

Appearance	Value For Money	Flavor
★☆☆☆☆	★☆☆☆☆	★☆☆☆☆

Would you try again?		Overall Rating
☐ YES	☐ NO	★☆☆☆☆

Cigar Tasting Journal

NAME			
BRAND		TYPE	
WRAPPER		FILLER	
ORIGIN		SAMPLED	

Label

CIGAR LABEL HERE

Flavor Meter

	VERY MILD	MILD	MEDIUM	MED-FULL	FULL
BODY					
FLAVOR					
STRENGTH					

Notes

Flavor Wheel

LEATHER, OILY, BITTER, SPICY, EARTHY, WOODY, NUTTY, CREAMY, CHOCOLATE, TOFFEE, SWEET, FLORAL, SOUR, TOASTED, FRUITY, HERBAL

Appearance	Value For Money	Flavor
★☆☆☆☆	★☆☆☆☆	★☆☆☆☆

Would you try again?	Overall Rating
☐ YES ☐ NO	★☆☆☆☆

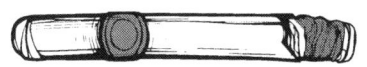

Cigar Tasting Journal

	NAME				
	BRAND			TYPE	
	WRAPPER			FILLER	
	ORIGIN			SAMPLED	

Label

CIGAR LABEL HERE

Flavor Meter

BODY	VERY MILD	MILD	MEDIUM	MED-FULL	FULL
FLAVOR	VERY MILD	MILD	MEDIUM	MED-FULL	FULL
STRENGTH	VERY MILD	MILD	MEDIUM	MED-FULL	FULL

Notes

Flavor Wheel

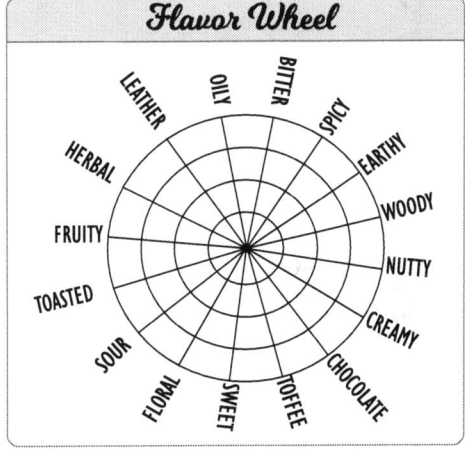

Flavors: LEATHER, OILY, BITTER, SPICY, EARTHY, WOODY, NUTTY, CREAMY, CHOCOLATE, TOFFEE, SWEET, FLORAL, SOUR, TOASTED, FRUITY, HERBAL

Appearance	Value For Money	Flavor
★☆☆☆☆	★☆☆☆☆	★☆☆☆☆

Would you try again?	Overall Rating
☐ YES ☐ NO	★☆☆☆☆

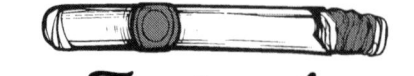

Cigar Tasting Journal

	NAME	
	BRAND	
	WRAPPER	
	ORIGIN	

	TYPE	
	FILLER	
	SAMPLED	

Label

Flavor Meter

BODY	VERY MILD	MILD	MEDIUM	MED-FULL	FULL
FLAVOR	VERY MILD	MILD	MEDIUM	MED-FULL	FULL
STRENGTH	VERY MILD	MILD	MEDIUM	MED-FULL	FULL

Notes

Flavor Wheel

Appearance	Value For Money	Flavor
★☆☆☆☆	★☆☆☆☆	★☆☆☆☆

Would you try again?		Overall Rating
☐ YES	☐ NO	★☆☆☆☆

Cigar Tasting Journal

	NAME				
	BRAND			TYPE	
	WRAPPER			FILLER	
	ORIGIN			SAMPLED	

Label

CIGAR LABEL HERE

Flavor Meter

	BODY	VERY MILD	MILD	MEDIUM	MED-FULL	FULL
	FLAVOR	VERY MILD	MILD	MEDIUM	MED-FULL	FULL
	STRENGTH	VERY MILD	MILD	MEDIUM	MED-FULL	FULL

Notes

Flavor Wheel

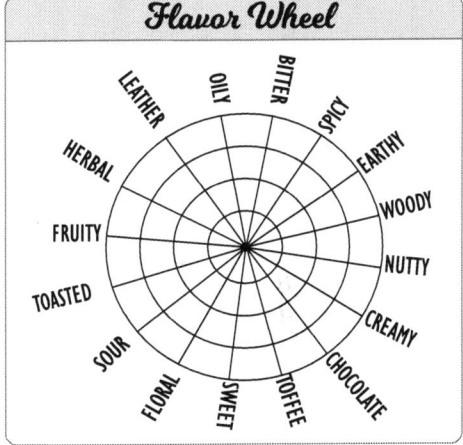

Appearance	Value For Money	Flavor
★☆☆☆☆	★☆☆☆☆	★☆☆☆☆

Would you try again?	Overall Rating
☐ YES ☐ NO	★☆☆☆☆

Cigar Tasting Journal

NAME			
BRAND		TYPE	
WRAPPER		FILLER	
ORIGIN		SAMPLED	

Label

Flavor Meter

	VERY MILD	MILD	MEDIUM	MED-FULL	FULL
BODY					
FLAVOR					
STRENGTH					

Notes

Flavor Wheel

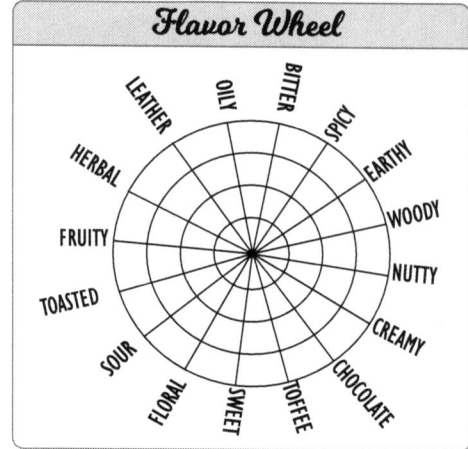

Appearance	Value For Money	Flavor
★☆☆☆☆	★☆☆☆☆	★☆☆☆☆

Would you try again?	Overall Rating
☐ YES ☐ NO	★☆☆☆☆

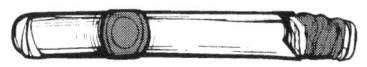

Cigar Tasting Journal

	NAME				
	BRAND			TYPE	
	WRAPPER			FILLER	
	ORIGIN			SAMPLED	

Label

CIGAR LABEL HERE

Flavor Meter

BODY	VERY MILD	MILD	MEDIUM	MED-FULL	FULL
FLAVOR	VERY MILD	MILD	MEDIUM	MED-FULL	FULL
STRENGTH	VERY MILD	MILD	MEDIUM	MED-FULL	FULL

Notes

Flavor Wheel

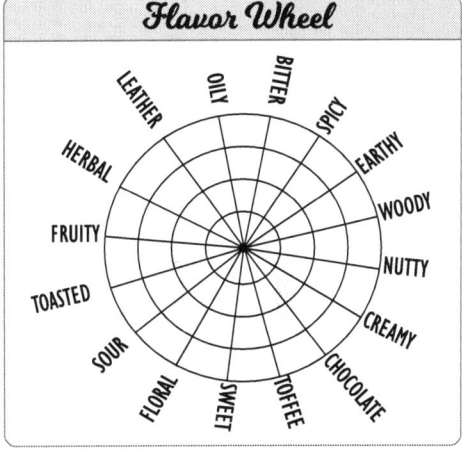

Appearance	Value For Money	Flavor
★☆☆☆☆	★☆☆☆☆	★☆☆☆☆

Would you try again?		Overall Rating
☐ YES	☐ NO	★☆☆☆☆

Cigar Tasting Journal

NAME				
BRAND		TYPE		
WRAPPER		FILLER		
ORIGIN		SAMPLED		

Label

Flavor Meter

	VERY MILD	MILD	MEDIUM	MED-FULL	FULL
BODY					
FLAVOR					
STRENGTH					

Notes

Flavor Wheel

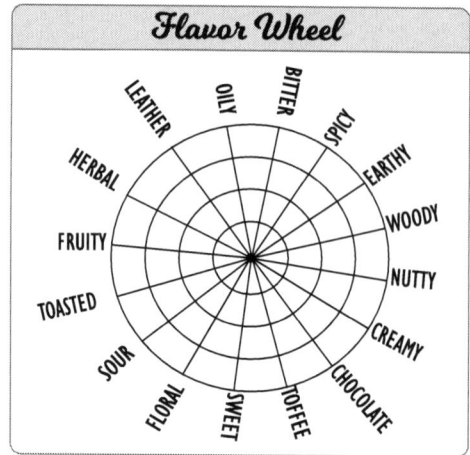

Appearance	Value For Money	Flavor
★☆☆☆☆	★☆☆☆☆	★☆☆☆☆

Would you try again?		Overall Rating
☐ YES	☐ NO	★☆☆☆☆

Cigar Tasting Journal

	NAME				TYPE	
	BRAND				FILLER	
	WRAPPER				SAMPLED	
	ORIGIN					

Label

CIGAR LABEL HERE

Flavor Meter

		VERY MILD	MILD	MEDIUM	MED-FULL	FULL
	BODY					
	FLAVOR					
	STRENGTH					

Notes

Flavor Wheel

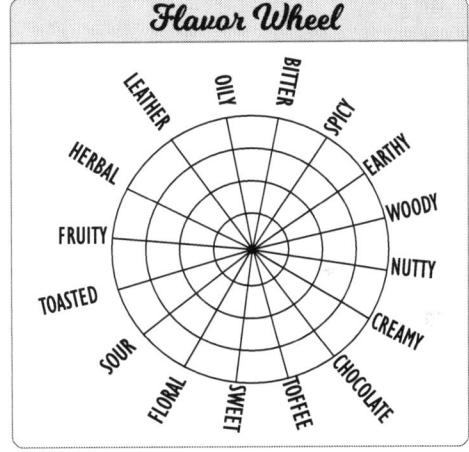

Appearance	Value For Money	Flavor
★☆☆☆☆	★☆☆☆☆	★☆☆☆☆

Would you try again?		Overall Rating
☐ YES	☐ NO	★☆☆☆☆

Cigar Tasting Journal

	NAME				
	BRAND			TYPE	
	WRAPPER			FILLER	
	ORIGIN			SAMPLED	

Label

Flavor Meter

		VERY MILD	MILD	MEDIUM	MED-FULL	FULL
	BODY					
	FLAVOR					
	STRENGTH					

Notes

Flavor Wheel

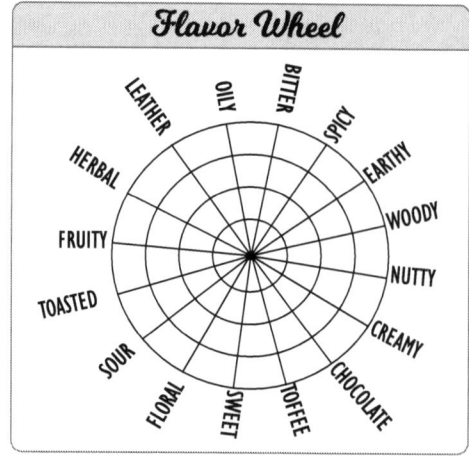

Appearance	Value For Money	Flavor
☆☆☆☆☆	☆☆☆☆☆	☆☆☆☆☆

Would you try again?	Overall Rating
☐ YES ☐ NO	☆☆☆☆☆

Cigar Tasting Journal

	NAME				TYPE	
	BRAND				FILLER	
	WRAPPER				SAMPLED	
	ORIGIN					

Label

CIGAR LABEL HERE

Flavor Meter

		VERY MILD	MILD	MEDIUM	MED-FULL	FULL
	BODY					
	FLAVOR					
	STRENGTH					

Notes

Flavor Wheel

Appearance	Value For Money	Flavor
★☆☆☆☆	★☆☆☆☆	★☆☆☆☆

Would you try again?		Overall Rating
☐ YES	☐ NO	★☆☆☆☆

Cigar Tasting Journal

	NAME	
	BRAND	
	WRAPPER	
	ORIGIN	

	TYPE	
	FILLER	
	SAMPLED	

Label

Flavor Meter

		VERY MILD	MILD	MEDIUM	MED-FULL	FULL
	BODY					
	FLAVOR					
	STRENGTH					

Notes

Flavor Wheel

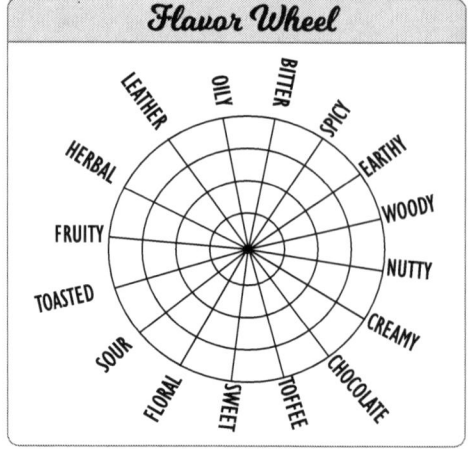

Appearance	Value For Money	Flavor
★☆☆☆☆	★☆☆☆☆	★☆☆☆☆

Would you try again?		Overall Rating
☐ YES	☐ NO	★☆☆☆☆

Cigar Tasting Journal

NAME		TYPE	
BRAND		FILLER	
WRAPPER		SAMPLED	
ORIGIN			

Label

CIGAR LABEL HERE

Flavor Meter

	VERY MILD	MILD	MEDIUM	MED-FULL	FULL
BODY					
FLAVOR					
STRENGTH					

Notes

Flavor Wheel

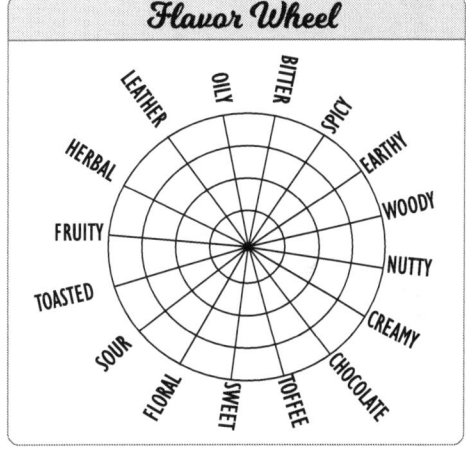

Appearance	Value For Money	Flavor
★☆☆☆☆	★☆☆☆☆	★☆☆☆☆

Would you try again?	Overall Rating
☐ YES ☐ NO	★☆☆☆☆

Cigar Tasting Journal

	NAME			TYPE	
	BRAND			FILLER	
	WRAPPER			SAMPLED	
	ORIGIN				

Label

Flavor Meter

		VERY MILD	MILD	MEDIUM	MED-FULL	FULL
	BODY					
	FLAVOR					
	STRENGTH					

Notes

Flavor Wheel

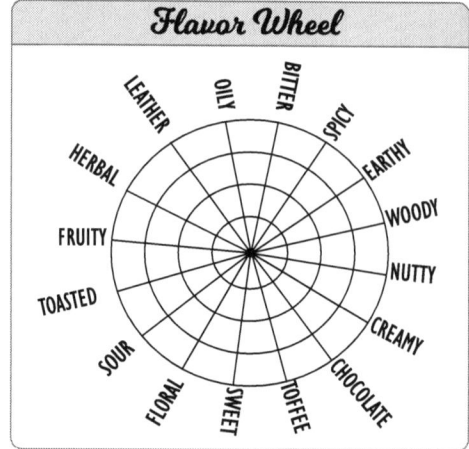

Appearance	Value For Money	Flavor
★☆☆☆☆	★☆☆☆☆	★☆☆☆☆

Would you try again?		Overall Rating
☐ YES	☐ NO	★☆☆☆☆

Cigar Tasting Journal

	NAME				
	BRAND			TYPE	
	WRAPPER			FILLER	
	ORIGIN			SAMPLED	

Label

CIGAR LABEL HERE

Flavor Meter

		VERY MILD	MILD	MEDIUM	MED-FULL	FULL
	BODY					
	FLAVOR					
	STRENGTH					

Notes

Flavor Wheel

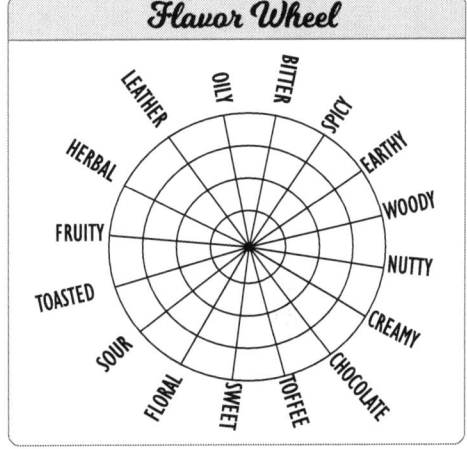

Appearance	Value For Money	Flavor
★☆☆☆☆	★☆☆☆☆	★☆☆☆☆

Would you try again?	Overall Rating
☐ YES ☐ NO	★☆☆☆☆

Cigar Tasting Journal

🚬	NAME			
	BRAND		TYPE	
	WRAPPER		FILLER	
🌐	ORIGIN		SAMPLED	

Label

Flavor Meter

		VERY MILD	MILD	MEDIUM	MED-FULL	FULL
	BODY	VERY MILD	MILD	MEDIUM	MED-FULL	FULL
	FLAVOR	VERY MILD	MILD	MEDIUM	MED-FULL	FULL
	STRENGTH	VERY MILD	MILD	MEDIUM	MED-FULL	FULL

Notes

Flavor Wheel

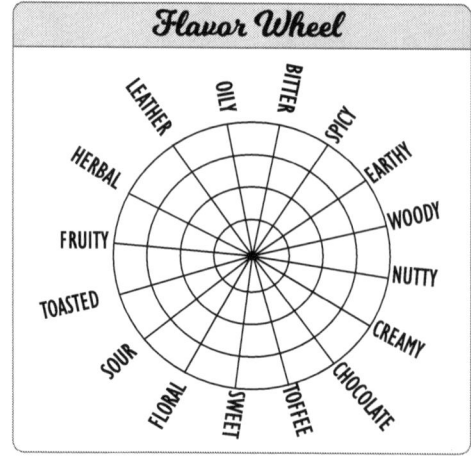

Appearance	Value For Money	Flavor
★☆☆☆☆	★☆☆☆☆	★☆☆☆☆

Would you try again?		Overall Rating
☐ YES	☐ NO	★☆☆☆☆

Cigar Tasting Journal

	NAME				
	BRAND			TYPE	
	WRAPPER			FILLER	
	ORIGIN			SAMPLED	

Label

Cigar Label Here

Flavor Meter

BODY	VERY MILD	MILD	MEDIUM	MED-FULL	FULL
FLAVOR	VERY MILD	MILD	MEDIUM	MED-FULL	FULL
STRENGTH	VERY MILD	MILD	MEDIUM	MED-FULL	FULL

Notes

Flavor Wheel

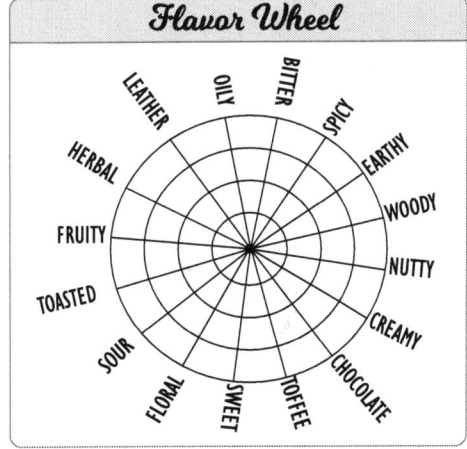

Appearance	Value For Money	Flavor
★☆☆☆☆	★☆☆☆☆	★☆☆☆☆

Would you try again?		Overall Rating
☐ YES	☐ NO	★☆☆☆☆

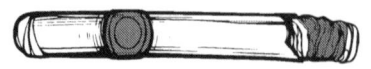

Cigar Tasting Journal

	NAME			
	BRAND		TYPE	
	WRAPPER		FILLER	
	ORIGIN		SAMPLED	

Label

Flavor Meter

		VERY MILD	MILD	MEDIUM	MED-FULL	FULL
	BODY					
	FLAVOR					
	STRENGTH					

Notes

Flavor Wheel

Appearance	Value For Money	Flavor
★☆☆☆☆	★☆☆☆☆	★☆☆☆☆

Would you try again?		Overall Rating
☐ YES	☐ NO	★☆☆☆☆

Cigar Tasting Journal

NAME				
BRAND		TYPE		
WRAPPER		FILLER		
ORIGIN		SAMPLED		

Label

CIGAR LABEL HERE

Flavor Meter

	VERY MILD	MILD	MEDIUM	MED-FULL	FULL
BODY					
FLAVOR					
STRENGTH					

Notes

Flavor Wheel

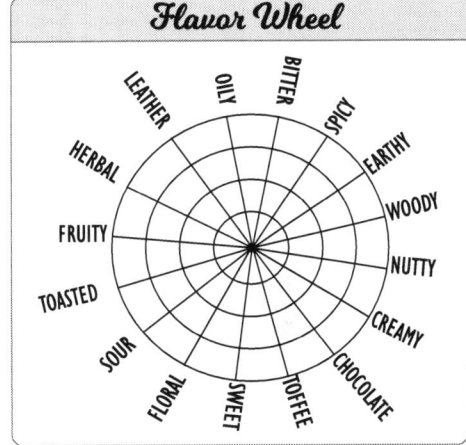

LEATHER · OILY · BITTER · SPICY · EARTHY · WOODY · NUTTY · CREAMY · CHOCOLATE · TOFFEE · SWEET · FLORAL · SOUR · TOASTED · FRUITY · HERBAL

Appearance	Value For Money	Flavor
★☆☆☆☆	★☆☆☆☆	★☆☆☆☆

Would you try again?	Overall Rating
☐ YES ☐ NO	★☆☆☆☆

Cigar Tasting Journal

NAME			
BRAND		TYPE	
WRAPPER		FILLER	
ORIGIN		SAMPLED	

Label

CIGAR LABEL HERE

Flavor Meter

	VERY MILD	MILD	MEDIUM	MED-FULL	FULL
BODY					
FLAVOR					
STRENGTH					

Notes

Flavor Wheel

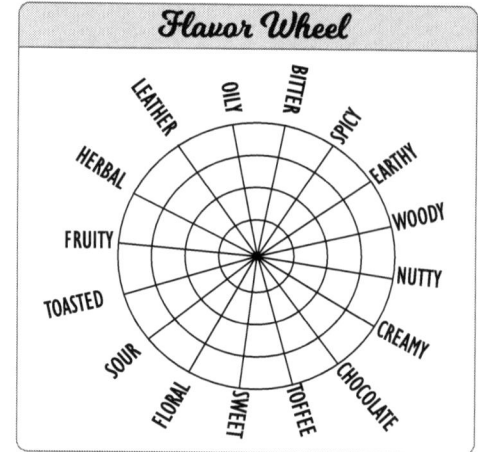

Appearance	Value For Money	Flavor
★☆☆☆☆	★☆☆☆☆	★☆☆☆☆

Would you try again?		Overall Rating
☐ YES	☐ NO	★☆☆☆☆

Cigar Tasting Journal

	NAME				
	BRAND			TYPE	
	WRAPPER			FILLER	
	ORIGIN			SAMPLED	

Label

CIGAR LABEL HERE

Flavor Meter

BODY	VERY MILD	MILD	MEDIUM	MED-FULL	FULL
FLAVOR	VERY MILD	MILD	MEDIUM	MED-FULL	FULL
STRENGTH	VERY MILD	MILD	MEDIUM	MED-FULL	FULL

Notes

Flavor Wheel

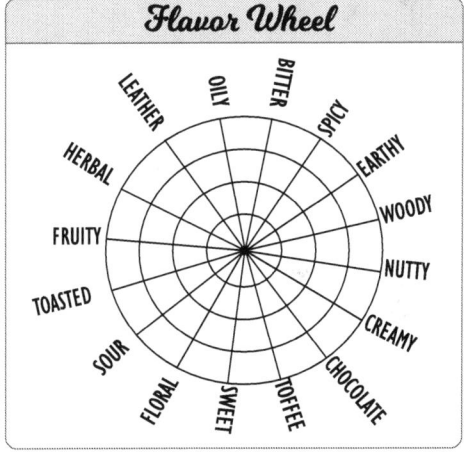

Appearance	Value For Money	Flavor
★☆☆☆☆	★☆☆☆☆	★☆☆☆☆

Would you try again?	Overall Rating
☐ YES ☐ NO	★☆☆☆☆

Cigar Tasting Journal

	NAME			TYPE	
	BRAND			FILLER	
	WRAPPER			SAMPLED	
	ORIGIN				

Label

Flavor Meter

	BODY	VERY MILD	MILD	MEDIUM	MED-FULL	FULL
	FLAVOR	VERY MILD	MILD	MEDIUM	MED-FULL	FULL
	STRENGTH	VERY MILD	MILD	MEDIUM	MED-FULL	FULL

Notes

Flavor Wheel

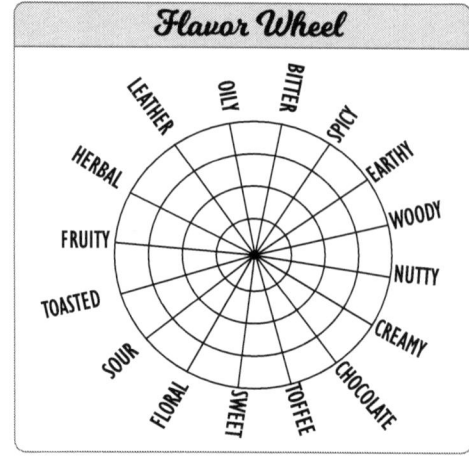

Appearance	Value For Money	Flavor
★☆☆☆☆	★☆☆☆☆	★☆☆☆☆

Would you try again?		Overall Rating
☐ YES	☐ NO	★☆☆☆☆

Cigar Tasting Journal

	NAME				
	BRAND			TYPE	
	WRAPPER			FILLER	
	ORIGIN			SAMPLED	

Label

CIGAR LABEL HERE

Flavor Meter

BODY	VERY MILD	MILD	MEDIUM	MED-FULL	FULL
FLAVOR	VERY MILD	MILD	MEDIUM	MED-FULL	FULL
STRENGTH	VERY MILD	MILD	MEDIUM	MED-FULL	FULL

Notes

Flavor Wheel

LEATHER, OILY, BITTER, SPICY, EARTHY, WOODY, NUTTY, CREAMY, CHOCOLATE, TOFFEE, SWEET, FLORAL, SOUR, TOASTED, FRUITY, HERBAL

Appearance	Value For Money	Flavor
★☆☆☆☆	★☆☆☆☆	★☆☆☆☆

Would you try again?	Overall Rating
☐ YES ☐ NO	★☆☆☆☆

Cigar Tasting Journal

	NAME				
	BRAND			TYPE	
	WRAPPER			FILLER	
	ORIGIN			SAMPLED	

Label

Flavor Meter

		VERY MILD	MILD	MEDIUM	MED-FULL	FULL
	BODY					
	FLAVOR					
	STRENGTH					

Notes

Flavor Wheel

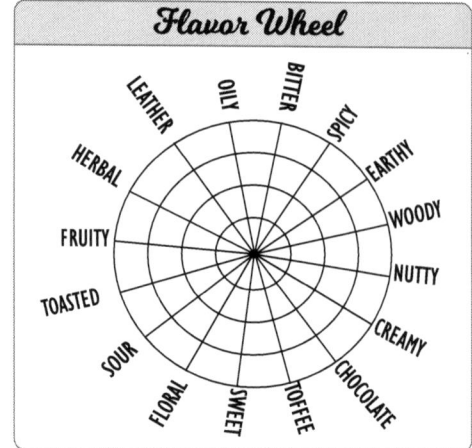

Appearance	Value For Money	Flavor
★☆☆☆☆	★☆☆☆☆	★☆☆☆☆

Would you try again?		Overall Rating
☐ YES	☐ NO	★☆☆☆☆

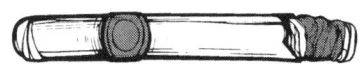

Cigar Tasting Journal

NAME				
BRAND		TYPE		
WRAPPER		FILLER		
ORIGIN		SAMPLED		

Label

Flavor Meter

	VERY MILD	MILD	MEDIUM	MED-FULL	FULL
BODY					
FLAVOR					
STRENGTH					

Notes

Flavor Wheel

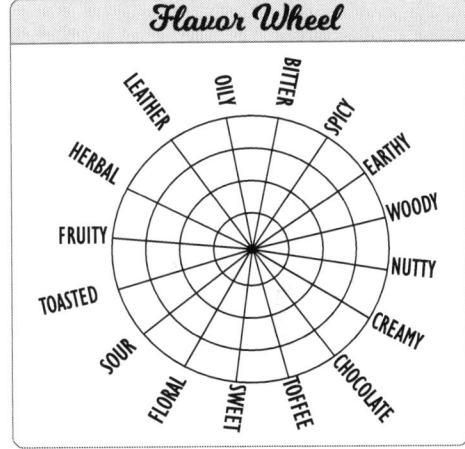

Appearance	Value For Money	Flavor
★☆☆☆☆	★☆☆☆☆	★☆☆☆☆

Would you try again?		Overall Rating
☐ YES	☐ NO	★☆☆☆☆

Cigar Tasting Journal

NAME			
BRAND		TYPE	
WRAPPER		FILLER	
ORIGIN		SAMPLED	

Label

CIGAR LABEL HERE

Flavor Meter

	VERY MILD	MILD	MEDIUM	MED-FULL	FULL
BODY					
FLAVOR					
STRENGTH					

Notes

Flavor Wheel

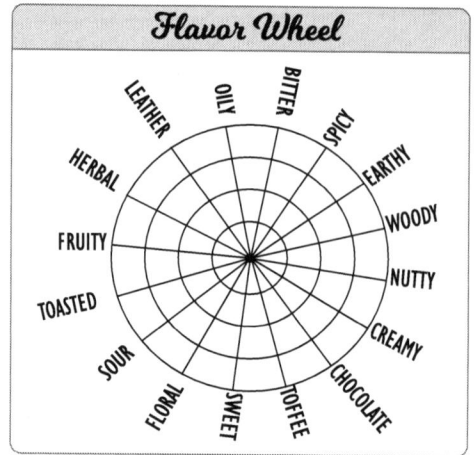

LEATHER · OILY · BITTER · SPICY · EARTHY · WOODY · NUTTY · CREAMY · CHOCOLATE · TOFFEE · SWEET · FLORAL · SOUR · TOASTED · FRUITY · HERBAL

Appearance	Value For Money	Flavor
☆☆☆☆☆	☆☆☆☆☆	☆☆☆☆☆

Would you try again?		Overall Rating
☐ YES	☐ NO	☆☆☆☆☆

Cigar Tasting Journal

NAME				
BRAND		TYPE		
WRAPPER		FILLER		
ORIGIN		SAMPLED		

Label

CIGAR LABEL HERE

Flavor Meter

BODY	VERY MILD	MILD	MEDIUM	MED-FULL	FULL
FLAVOR	VERY MILD	MILD	MEDIUM	MED-FULL	FULL
STRENGTH	VERY MILD	MILD	MEDIUM	MED-FULL	FULL

Notes

Flavor Wheel

Appearance	Value For Money	Flavor
★☆☆☆☆	★☆☆☆☆	★☆☆☆☆

Would you try again?		Overall Rating
☐ YES	☐ NO	★☆☆☆☆

Cigar Tasting Journal

	NAME			TYPE	
	BRAND			FILLER	
	WRAPPER			SAMPLED	
	ORIGIN				

Label

CIGAR LABEL HERE

Flavor Meter

	BODY	VERY MILD	MILD	MEDIUM	MED-FULL	FULL
	FLAVOR	VERY MILD	MILD	MEDIUM	MED-FULL	FULL
	STRENGTH	VERY MILD	MILD	MEDIUM	MED-FULL	FULL

Notes

Flavor Wheel

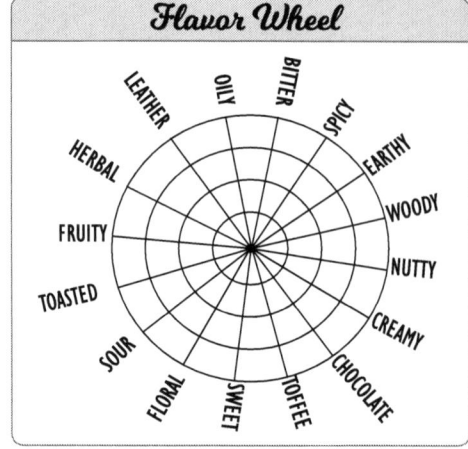

Appearance	Value For Money	Flavor
★☆☆☆☆	★☆☆☆☆	★☆☆☆☆

Would you try again?		Overall Rating
☐ YES	☐ NO	★☆☆☆☆

Cigar Tasting Journal

	NAME			
	BRAND		TYPE	
	WRAPPER		FILLER	
	ORIGIN		SAMPLED	

Label

Flavor Meter

BODY	VERY MILD	MILD	MEDIUM	MED-FULL	FULL
FLAVOR	VERY MILD	MILD	MEDIUM	MED-FULL	FULL
STRENGTH	VERY MILD	MILD	MEDIUM	MED-FULL	FULL

Notes

Flavor Wheel

Appearance	Value For Money	Flavor
★☆☆☆☆	★☆☆☆☆	★☆☆☆☆

Would you try again?		Overall Rating
☐ YES	☐ NO	★☆☆☆☆

Cigar Tasting Journal

	NAME				
	BRAND			TYPE	
	WRAPPER			FILLER	
	ORIGIN			SAMPLED	

Label

Flavor Meter

	BODY	VERY MILD	MILD	MEDIUM	MED-FULL	FULL
	FLAVOR	VERY MILD	MILD	MEDIUM	MED-FULL	FULL
	STRENGTH	VERY MILD	MILD	MEDIUM	MED-FULL	FULL

Notes

Flavor Wheel

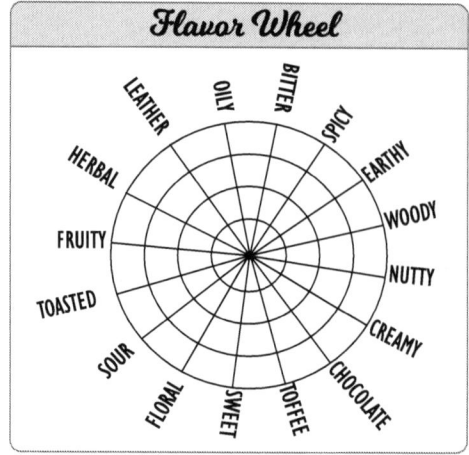

Appearance	Value For Money	Flavor
★☆☆☆☆	★☆☆☆☆	★☆☆☆☆

Would you try again?		Overall Rating
☐ YES	☐ NO	★☆☆☆☆

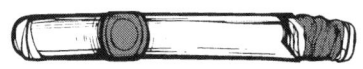

Cigar Tasting Journal

	NAME			
	BRAND		TYPE	
	WRAPPER		FILLER	
	ORIGIN		SAMPLED	

Label

CIGAR LABEL HERE

Flavor Meter

BODY	VERY MILD	MILD	MEDIUM	MED-FULL	FULL
FLAVOR	VERY MILD	MILD	MEDIUM	MED-FULL	FULL
STRENGTH	VERY MILD	MILD	MEDIUM	MED-FULL	FULL

Notes

Flavor Wheel

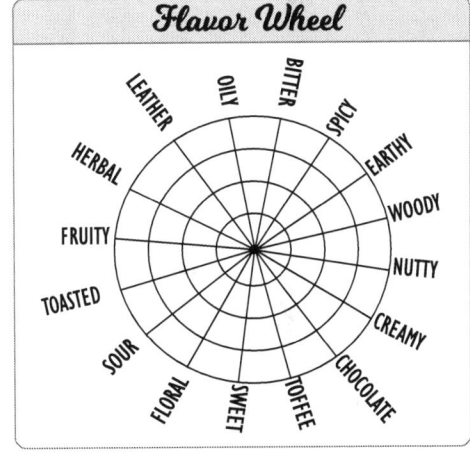

Appearance	Value For Money	Flavor
★☆☆☆☆	★☆☆☆☆	★☆☆☆☆

Would you try again?	Overall Rating
☐ YES ☐ NO	★☆☆☆☆

Cigar Tasting Journal

	NAME				
	BRAND			TYPE	
	WRAPPER			FILLER	
	ORIGIN			SAMPLED	

Label

Flavor Meter

BODY	VERY MILD	MILD	MEDIUM	MED-FULL	FULL
FLAVOR	VERY MILD	MILD	MEDIUM	MED-FULL	FULL
STRENGTH	VERY MILD	MILD	MEDIUM	MED-FULL	FULL

Notes

Flavor Wheel

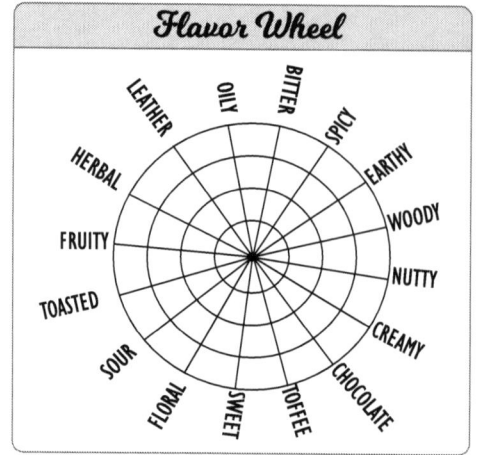

Appearance	Value For Money	Flavor
☆☆☆☆☆	☆☆☆☆☆	☆☆☆☆☆

Would you try again?		Overall Rating
☐ YES	☐ NO	☆☆☆☆☆

Cigar Tasting Journal

NAME			
BRAND		TYPE	
WRAPPER		FILLER	
ORIGIN		SAMPLED	

Label

CIGAR LABEL HERE

Flavor Meter

	VERY MILD	MILD	MEDIUM	MED-FULL	FULL
BODY					
FLAVOR					
STRENGTH					

Notes

Flavor Wheel

Appearance	Value For Money	Flavor
★☆☆☆☆	★☆☆☆☆	★☆☆☆☆

Would you try again?		Overall Rating
☐ YES	☐ NO	★☆☆☆☆

Cigar Tasting Journal

NAME				
BRAND		TYPE		
WRAPPER		FILLER		
ORIGIN		SAMPLED		

Label

Flavor Meter

BODY	VERY MILD	MILD	MEDIUM	MED-FULL	FULL
FLAVOR	VERY MILD	MILD	MEDIUM	MED-FULL	FULL
STRENGTH	VERY MILD	MILD	MEDIUM	MED-FULL	FULL

Notes

Flavor Wheel

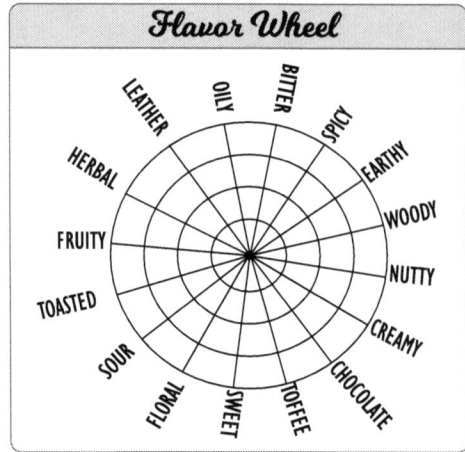

Appearance	Value For Money	Flavor
★☆☆☆☆	★☆☆☆☆	★☆☆☆☆

Would you try again?		Overall Rating
☐ YES	☐ NO	★☆☆☆☆

Cigar Tasting Journal

	NAME			TYPE	
	BRAND			FILLER	
	WRAPPER			SAMPLED	
	ORIGIN				

Label

CIGAR LABEL HERE

Flavor Meter

	BODY	VERY MILD	MILD	MEDIUM	MED-FULL	FULL
	FLAVOR	VERY MILD	MILD	MEDIUM	MED-FULL	FULL
	STRENGTH	VERY MILD	MILD	MEDIUM	MED-FULL	FULL

Notes

Flavor Wheel

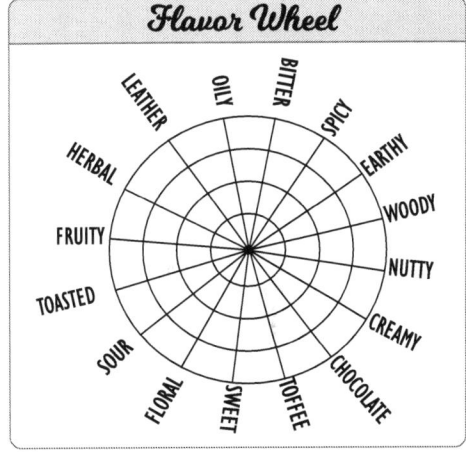

Appearance	Value For Money	Flavor
★☆☆☆☆	★☆☆☆☆	★☆☆☆☆

Would you try again?		Overall Rating
☐ YES	☐ NO	★☆☆☆☆

Cigar Tasting Journal

	NAME				
	BRAND			TYPE	
	WRAPPER			FILLER	
	ORIGIN			SAMPLED	

Label

CIGAR LABEL HERE

Flavor Meter

	BODY	VERY MILD	MILD	MEDIUM	MED-FULL	FULL
	FLAVOR	VERY MILD	MILD	MEDIUM	MED-FULL	FULL
	STRENGTH	VERY MILD	MILD	MEDIUM	MED-FULL	FULL

Notes

Flavor Wheel

LEATHER, OILY, BITTER, SPICY, EARTHY, WOODY, NUTTY, CREAMY, CHOCOLATE, TOFFEE, SWEET, FLORAL, SOUR, TOASTED, FRUITY, HERBAL

Appearance	Value For Money	Flavor
★☆☆☆☆	★☆☆☆☆	★☆☆☆☆

Would you try again?		Overall Rating
☐ YES	☐ NO	★☆☆☆☆

Cigar Tasting Journal

	NAME				
	BRAND			TYPE	
	WRAPPER			FILLER	
	ORIGIN			SAMPLED	

Label

CIGAR LABEL HERE

Flavor Meter

		VERY MILD	MILD	MEDIUM	MED-FULL	FULL
	BODY					
	FLAVOR					
	STRENGTH					

Notes

Flavor Wheel

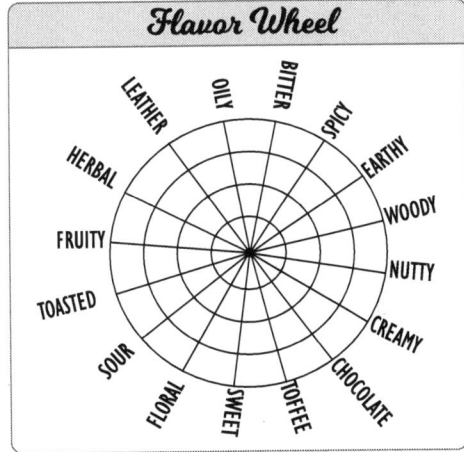

Appearance	Value For Money	Flavor
☆☆☆☆☆	☆☆☆☆☆	☆☆☆☆☆

Would you try again?		Overall Rating
☐ YES	☐ NO	☆☆☆☆☆

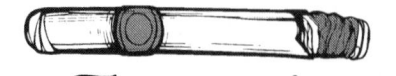

Cigar Tasting Journal

	NAME				
	BRAND			TYPE	
	WRAPPER			FILLER	
	ORIGIN			SAMPLED	

Label

CIGAR LABEL HERE

Flavor Meter

		VERY MILD	MILD	MEDIUM	MED-FULL	FULL
	BODY	VERY MILD	MILD	MEDIUM	MED-FULL	FULL
	FLAVOR	VERY MILD	MILD	MEDIUM	MED-FULL	FULL
	STRENGTH	VERY MILD	MILD	MEDIUM	MED-FULL	FULL

Notes

Flavor Wheel

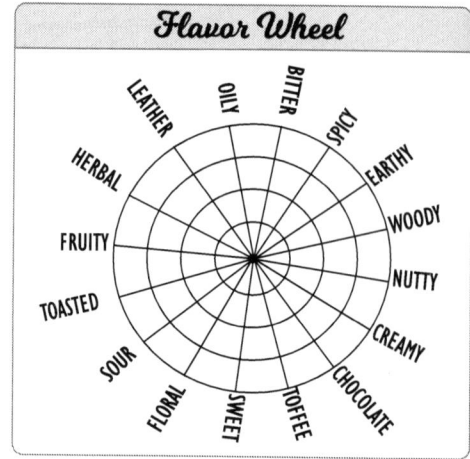

Appearance	Value For Money	Flavor
★☆☆☆☆	★☆☆☆☆	★☆☆☆☆

Would you try again?		Overall Rating
☐ YES	☐ NO	★☆☆☆☆

Cigar Tasting Journal

NAME				
BRAND		TYPE		
WRAPPER		FILLER		
ORIGIN		SAMPLED		

Label

Flavor Meter

	VERY MILD	MILD	MEDIUM	MED-FULL	FULL
BODY					
FLAVOR					
STRENGTH					

Notes

Flavor Wheel

LEATHER, OILY, BITTER, SPICY, EARTHY, WOODY, NUTTY, CREAMY, CHOCOLATE, TOFFEE, SWEET, FLORAL, SOUR, TOASTED, FRUITY, HERBAL

Appearance	Value For Money	Flavor
★☆☆☆☆	★☆☆☆☆	★☆☆☆☆

Would you try again?	Overall Rating
☐ YES ☐ NO	★☆☆☆☆

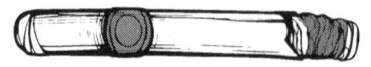

Cigar Tasting Journal

	NAME				
	BRAND			TYPE	
	WRAPPER			FILLER	
	ORIGIN			SAMPLED	

Label

CIGAR LABEL HERE

Flavor Meter

		VERY MILD	MILD	MEDIUM	MED-FULL	FULL
	BODY					
	FLAVOR					
	STRENGTH					

Notes

Flavor Wheel

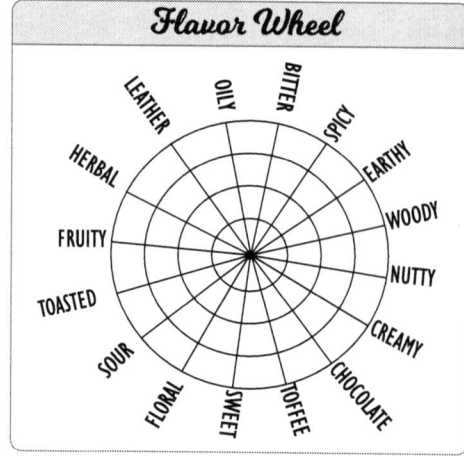

Appearance	Value For Money	Flavor
★☆☆☆☆	★☆☆☆☆	★☆☆☆☆

Would you try again?		Overall Rating
☐ YES	☐ NO	★☆☆☆☆

Cigar Tasting Journal

	NAME			
	BRAND		TYPE	
	WRAPPER		FILLER	
	ORIGIN		SAMPLED	

Label

CIGAR LABEL HERE

Flavor Meter

		VERY MILD	MILD	MEDIUM	MED-FULL	FULL
	BODY					
	FLAVOR					
	STRENGTH					

Notes

Flavor Wheel

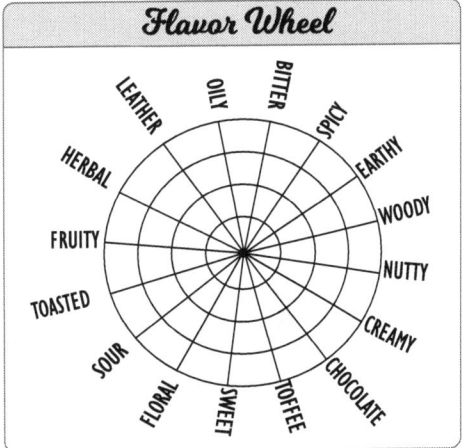

BITTER, OILY, SPICY, LEATHER, EARTHY, HERBAL, WOODY, FRUITY, NUTTY, TOASTED, CREAMY, SOUR, CHOCOLATE, FLORAL, SWEET, TOFFEE

Appearance	Value For Money	Flavor
★☆☆☆☆	★☆☆☆☆	★☆☆☆☆

Would you try again?		Overall Rating
☐ YES	☐ NO	★☆☆☆☆

Cigar Tasting Journal

NAME				
BRAND		TYPE		
WRAPPER		FILLER		
ORIGIN		SAMPLED		

Label

CIGAR LABEL HERE

Flavor Meter

	VERY MILD	MILD	MEDIUM	MED-FULL	FULL
BODY					
FLAVOR					
STRENGTH					

Notes

Flavor Wheel

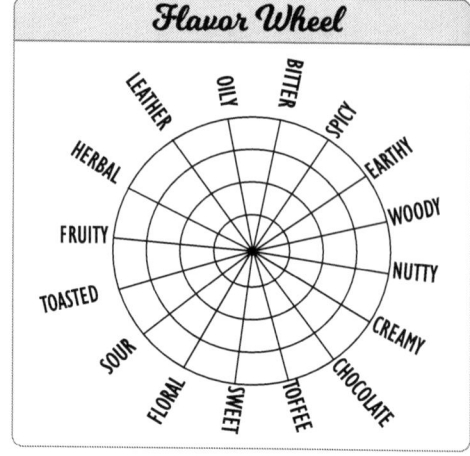

Appearance	Value For Money	Flavor
★☆☆☆☆	★☆☆☆☆	★☆☆☆☆

Would you try again?		Overall Rating
☐ YES	☐ NO	★☆☆☆☆

Cigar Tasting Journal

	NAME	
	BRAND	
	WRAPPER	
	ORIGIN	

	TYPE	
	FILLER	
	SAMPLED	

Label

CIGAR LABEL HERE

Flavor Meter

BODY	VERY MILD	MILD	MEDIUM	MED-FULL	FULL
FLAVOR	VERY MILD	MILD	MEDIUM	MED-FULL	FULL
STRENGTH	VERY MILD	MILD	MEDIUM	MED-FULL	FULL

Notes

Flavor Wheel

Bitter, Oily, Leather, Spicy, Herbal, Earthy, Woody, Fruity, Nutty, Toasted, Creamy, Sour, Chocolate, Floral, Sweet, Toffee

Appearance	Value For Money	Flavor
★☆☆☆☆	★☆☆☆☆	★☆☆☆☆

Would you try again?	Overall Rating
☐ YES ☐ NO	★☆☆☆☆

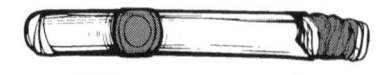

Cigar Tasting Journal

NAME			
BRAND		TYPE	
WRAPPER		FILLER	
ORIGIN		SAMPLED	

Label

CIGAR LABEL HERE

Flavor Meter

	VERY MILD	MILD	MEDIUM	MED-FULL	FULL
BODY					
FLAVOR					
STRENGTH					

Notes

Flavor Wheel

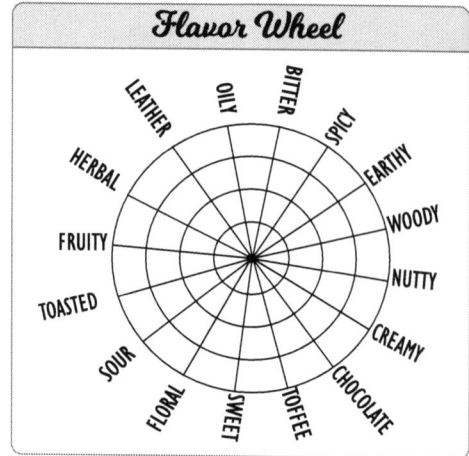

Appearance	Value For Money	Flavor
★☆☆☆☆	★☆☆☆☆	★☆☆☆☆

Would you try again?		Overall Rating
☐ YES	☐ NO	★☆☆☆☆

Cigar Tasting Journal

NAME			
BRAND		TYPE	
WRAPPER		FILLER	
ORIGIN		SAMPLED	

Label

CIGAR LABEL HERE

Flavor Meter

	VERY MILD	MILD	MEDIUM	MED-FULL	FULL
BODY					
FLAVOR					
STRENGTH					

Notes

Flavor Wheel

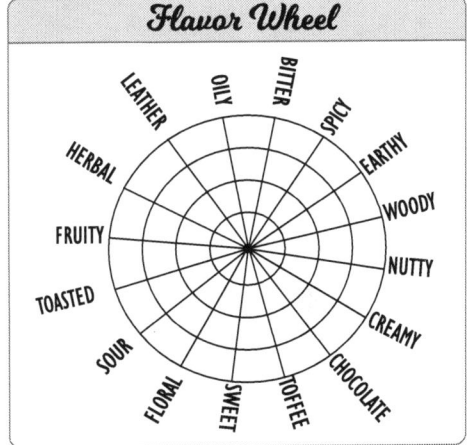

LEATHER, OILY, BITTER, SPICY, EARTHY, WOODY, NUTTY, CREAMY, CHOCOLATE, TOFFEE, SWEET, FLORAL, SOUR, TOASTED, FRUITY, HERBAL

Appearance	Value For Money	Flavor
★☆☆☆☆	★☆☆☆☆	★☆☆☆☆

Would you try again?	Overall Rating
☐ YES ☐ NO	★☆☆☆☆

Cigar Tasting Journal

	NAME				
	BRAND			TYPE	
	WRAPPER			FILLER	
	ORIGIN			SAMPLED	

Label

Flavor Meter

		VERY MILD	MILD	MEDIUM	MED-FULL	FULL
	BODY					
	FLAVOR					
	STRENGTH					

Notes

Flavor Wheel

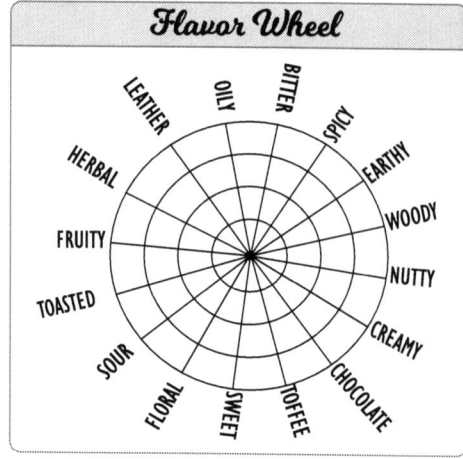

LEATHER · OILY · BITTER · SPICY · EARTHY · WOODY · NUTTY · CREAMY · CHOCOLATE · TOFFEE · SWEET · FLORAL · SOUR · TOASTED · FRUITY · HERBAL

Appearance	Value For Money	Flavor
★☆☆☆☆	★☆☆☆☆	★☆☆☆☆

Would you try again?	Overall Rating
☐ YES ☐ NO	★☆☆☆☆

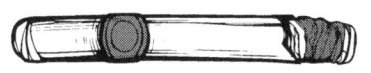

Cigar Tasting Journal

	NAME				
	BRAND			TYPE	
	WRAPPER			FILLER	
	ORIGIN			SAMPLED	

Label

CIGAR LABEL HERE

Flavor Meter

		VERY MILD	MILD	MEDIUM	MED-FULL	FULL
	BODY					
	FLAVOR					
	STRENGTH					

Notes

Flavor Wheel

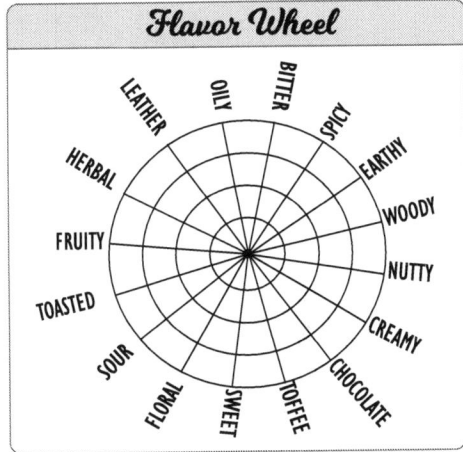

Appearance	Value For Money	Flavor
★☆☆☆☆	★☆☆☆☆	★☆☆☆☆

Would you try again?	Overall Rating
☐ YES ☐ NO	★☆☆☆☆

Cigar Tasting Journal

	NAME	
	BRAND	
	WRAPPER	
	ORIGIN	

	TYPE	
	FILLER	
	SAMPLED	

Label

CIGAR LABEL HERE

Flavor Meter

		VERY MILD	MILD	MEDIUM	MED-FULL	FULL
	BODY					
	FLAVOR					
	STRENGTH					

Notes

Flavor Wheel

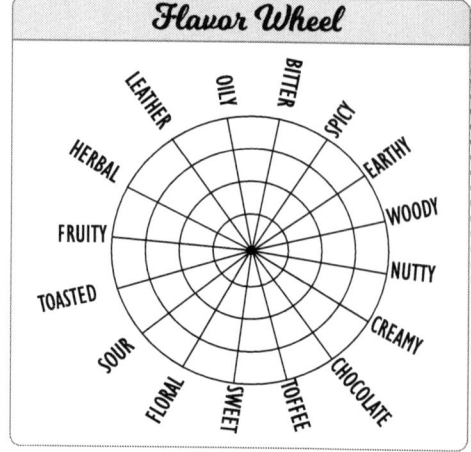

LEATHER · OILY · BITTER · SPICY · EARTHY · WOODY · NUTTY · CREAMY · CHOCOLATE · TOFFEE · SWEET · FLORAL · SOUR · TOASTED · FRUITY · HERBAL

Appearance	Value For Money	Flavor
★☆☆☆☆	★☆☆☆☆	★☆☆☆☆

Would you try again?	Overall Rating
☐ YES ☐ NO	★☆☆☆☆

Cigar Tasting Journal

NAME			
BRAND		TYPE	
WRAPPER		FILLER	
ORIGIN		SAMPLED	

Label

Flavor Meter

	VERY MILD	MILD	MEDIUM	MED-FULL	FULL
BODY					
FLAVOR					
STRENGTH					

Notes

Flavor Wheel

Flavors: LEATHER, OILY, BITTER, SPICY, EARTHY, WOODY, NUTTY, CREAMY, CHOCOLATE, TOFFEE, SWEET, FLORAL, SOUR, TOASTED, FRUITY, HERBAL

Appearance	Value For Money	Flavor
★☆☆☆☆	★☆☆☆☆	★☆☆☆☆

Would you try again?		Overall Rating
☐ YES	☐ NO	★☆☆☆☆

Cigar Tasting Journal

NAME			
BRAND		TYPE	
WRAPPER		FILLER	
ORIGIN		SAMPLED	

Label

CIGAR LABEL HERE

Flavor Meter

	VERY MILD	MILD	MEDIUM	MED-FULL	FULL
BODY					
FLAVOR					
STRENGTH					

Notes

Flavor Wheel

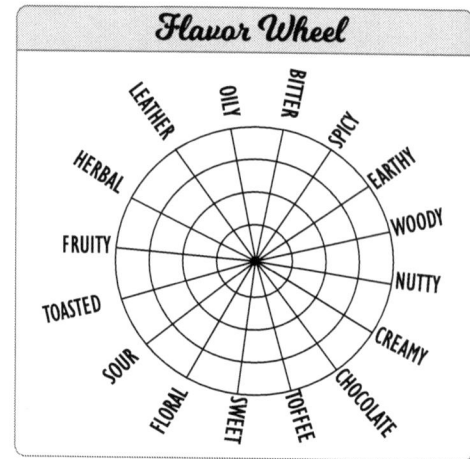

LEATHER · OILY · BITTER · SPICY · EARTHY · WOODY · NUTTY · CREAMY · CHOCOLATE · TOFFEE · SWEET · FLORAL · SOUR · TOASTED · FRUITY · HERBAL

Appearance	Value For Money	Flavor
★☆☆☆☆	★☆☆☆☆	★☆☆☆☆

Would you try again?		Overall Rating
☐ YES	☐ NO	★☆☆☆☆

Cigar Tasting Journal

	NAME				
	BRAND			TYPE	
	WRAPPER			FILLER	
	ORIGIN			SAMPLED	

Label

CIGAR LABEL HERE

Flavor Meter

		VERY MILD	MILD	MEDIUM	MED-FULL	FULL
	BODY					
	FLAVOR					
	STRENGTH					

Notes

Flavor Wheel

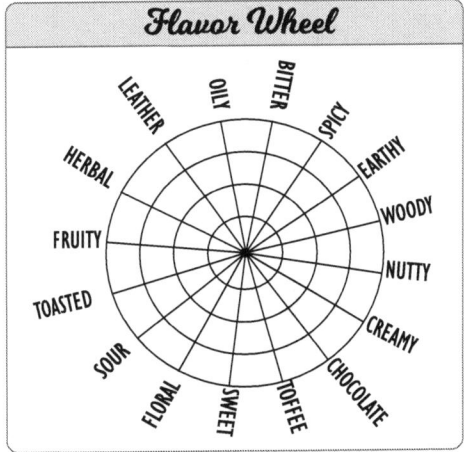

Appearance	Value For Money	Flavor
☆☆☆☆☆	☆☆☆☆☆	☆☆☆☆☆

Would you try again?	Overall Rating
☐ YES ☐ NO	☆☆☆☆☆

Cigar Tasting Journal

	NAME			TYPE	
	BRAND			FILLER	
	WRAPPER			SAMPLED	
	ORIGIN				

Label

CIGAR LABEL HERE

Flavor Meter

		VERY MILD	MILD	MEDIUM	MED-FULL	FULL
	BODY					
	FLAVOR					
	STRENGTH					

Notes

Flavor Wheel

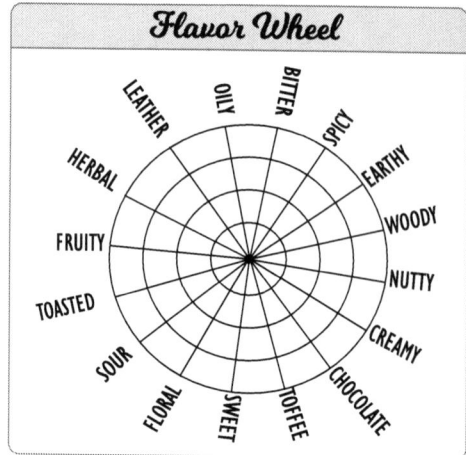

Appearance	Value For Money	Flavor
★☆☆☆☆	★☆☆☆☆	★☆☆☆☆

Would you try again?		Overall Rating
☐ YES	☐ NO	★☆☆☆☆

Cigar Tasting Journal

NAME	
BRAND		TYPE	
WRAPPER		FILLER	
ORIGIN		SAMPLED	

Label

CIGAR LABEL HERE

Flavor Meter

	VERY MILD	MILD	MEDIUM	MED-FULL	FULL
BODY					
FLAVOR					
STRENGTH					

Notes

Flavor Wheel

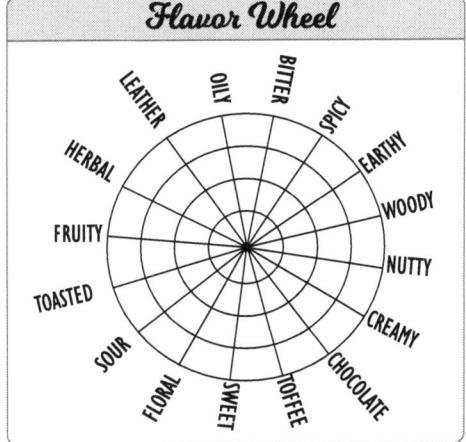

LEATHER, OILY, BITTER, SPICY, EARTHY, WOODY, NUTTY, CREAMY, CHOCOLATE, TOFFEE, SWEET, FLORAL, SOUR, TOASTED, FRUITY, HERBAL

Appearance	Value For Money	Flavor
★☆☆☆☆	★☆☆☆☆	★☆☆☆☆

Would you try again?	Overall Rating
☐ YES ☐ NO	★☆☆☆☆

Cigar Tasting Journal

	NAME				
	BRAND			TYPE	
	WRAPPER			FILLER	
	ORIGIN			SAMPLED	

Label

Flavor Meter

		VERY MILD	MILD	MEDIUM	MED-FULL	FULL
	BODY					
	FLAVOR					
	STRENGTH					

Notes

Flavor Wheel

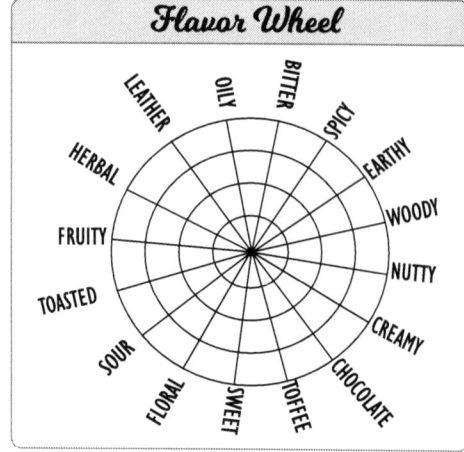

Appearance	Value For Money	Flavor
★☆☆☆☆	★☆☆☆☆	★☆☆☆☆

Would you try again?	Overall Rating
☐ YES ☐ NO	★☆☆☆☆

Cigar Tasting Journal

	NAME				
	BRAND			TYPE	
	WRAPPER			FILLER	
	ORIGIN			SAMPLED	

Label

CIGAR LABEL HERE

Flavor Meter

BODY	VERY MILD	MILD	MEDIUM	MED-FULL	FULL
FLAVOR	VERY MILD	MILD	MEDIUM	MED-FULL	FULL
STRENGTH	VERY MILD	MILD	MEDIUM	MED-FULL	FULL

Notes

Flavor Wheel

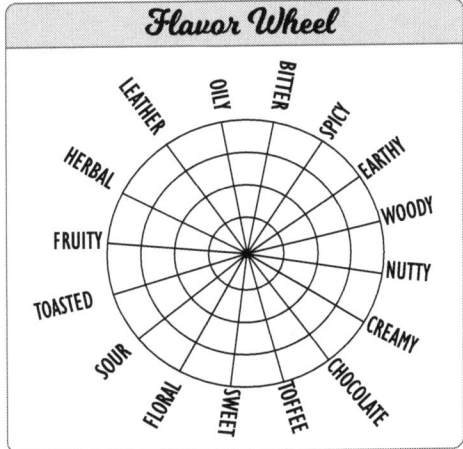

Appearance	Value For Money	Flavor
★☆☆☆☆	★☆☆☆☆	★☆☆☆☆

Would you try again?		Overall Rating
☐ YES	☐ NO	★☆☆☆☆

Cigar Tasting Journal

	NAME	
	BRAND	
	WRAPPER	
	ORIGIN	

	TYPE	
	FILLER	
	SAMPLED	

Label

CIGAR LABEL HERE

Flavor Meter

		VERY MILD	MILD	MEDIUM	MED-FULL	FULL
	BODY					
	FLAVOR					
	STRENGTH					

Notes

Flavor Wheel

LEATHER, OILY, BITTER, SPICY, EARTHY, WOODY, NUTTY, CREAMY, CHOCOLATE, TOFFEE, SWEET, FLORAL, SOUR, TOASTED, FRUITY, HERBAL

Appearance	Value For Money	Flavor
★☆☆☆☆	★☆☆☆☆	★☆☆☆☆

Would you try again?		Overall Rating
☐ YES	☐ NO	★☆☆☆☆

Cigar Tasting Journal

NAME	
BRAND	
WRAPPER	
ORIGIN	
TYPE	
FILLER	
SAMPLED	

Label

CIGAR LABEL HERE

Flavor Meter

	VERY MILD	MILD	MEDIUM	MED-FULL	FULL
BODY					
FLAVOR					
STRENGTH					

Notes

Flavor Wheel

Leather, Oily, Bitter, Spicy, Earthy, Woody, Nutty, Creamy, Chocolate, Toffee, Sweet, Floral, Sour, Toasted, Fruity, Herbal

Appearance	Value For Money	Flavor
☆☆☆☆☆	☆☆☆☆☆	☆☆☆☆☆

Would you try again?	Overall Rating
☐ YES ☐ NO	☆☆☆☆☆

Cigar Tasting Journal

	NAME				
	BRAND			TYPE	
	WRAPPER			FILLER	
	ORIGIN			SAMPLED	

Label

Flavor Meter

		VERY MILD	MILD	MEDIUM	MED-FULL	FULL
	BODY					
	FLAVOR					
	STRENGTH					

Notes

Flavor Wheel

Appearance	Value For Money	Flavor
★☆☆☆☆	★☆☆☆☆	★☆☆☆☆

Would you try again?	Overall Rating
☐ YES ☐ NO	★☆☆☆☆

Cigar Tasting Journal

NAME				
BRAND		TYPE		
WRAPPER		FILLER		
ORIGIN		SAMPLED		

Label

CIGAR LABEL HERE

Flavor Meter

	VERY MILD	MILD	MEDIUM	MED-FULL	FULL
BODY					
FLAVOR					
STRENGTH					

Notes

Flavor Wheel

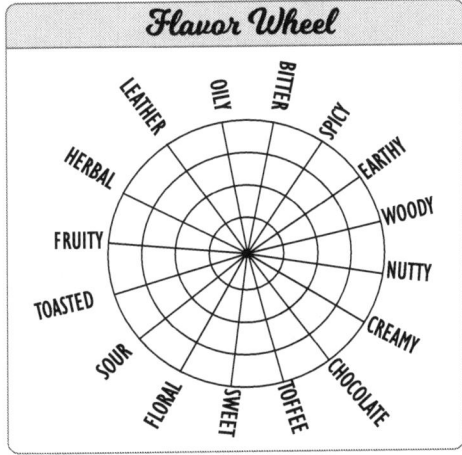

Appearance	Value For Money	Flavor
★☆☆☆☆	★☆☆☆☆	★☆☆☆☆

Would you try again?	Overall Rating
☐ YES ☐ NO	★☆☆☆☆

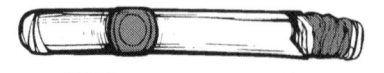

Cigar Tasting Journal

	NAME	
	BRAND	
	WRAPPER	
	ORIGIN	

	TYPE	
	FILLER	
	SAMPLED	

Label

CIGAR LABEL HERE

Flavor Meter

	BODY	VERY MILD	MILD	MEDIUM	MED-FULL	FULL
	FLAVOR	VERY MILD	MILD	MEDIUM	MED-FULL	FULL
	STRENGTH	VERY MILD	MILD	MEDIUM	MED-FULL	FULL

Notes

Flavor Wheel

Appearance	Value For Money	Flavor
★☆☆☆☆	★☆☆☆☆	★☆☆☆☆

Would you try again?		Overall Rating
☐ YES	☐ NO	★☆☆☆☆

Cigar Tasting Journal

	NAME				
	BRAND			TYPE	
	WRAPPER			FILLER	
	ORIGIN			SAMPLED	

Label

CIGAR LABEL HERE

Flavor Meter

BODY	VERY MILD	MILD	MEDIUM	MED-FULL	FULL
FLAVOR	VERY MILD	MILD	MEDIUM	MED-FULL	FULL
STRENGTH	VERY MILD	MILD	MEDIUM	MED-FULL	FULL

Notes

Flavor Wheel

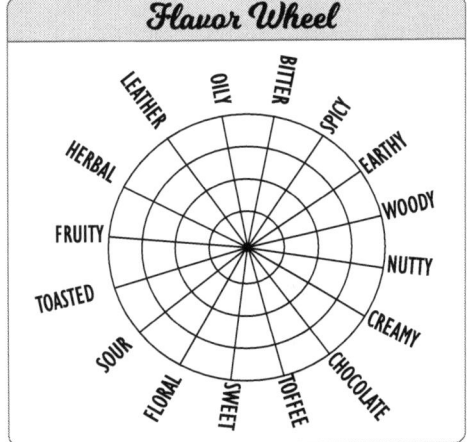

Appearance	Value For Money	Flavor
★☆☆☆☆	★☆☆☆☆	★☆☆☆☆

Would you try again?	Overall Rating
☐ YES ☐ NO	★☆☆☆☆

Cigar Tasting Journal

	NAME	
	BRAND	
	WRAPPER	
	ORIGIN	

	TYPE	
	FILLER	
	SAMPLED	

Label

CIGAR LABEL HERE

Flavor Meter

		VERY MILD	MILD	MEDIUM	MED-FULL	FULL
	BODY					
	FLAVOR					
	STRENGTH					

Notes

Flavor Wheel

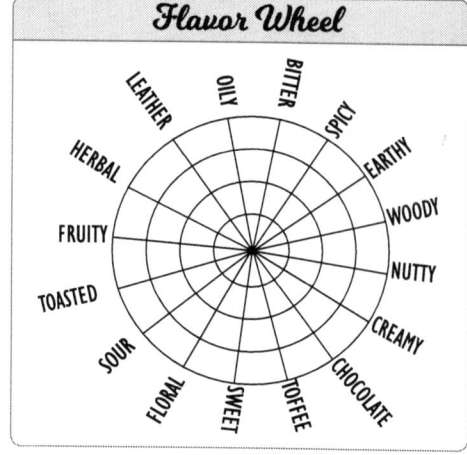

LEATHER, OILY, BITTER, SPICY, EARTHY, WOODY, NUTTY, CREAMY, CHOCOLATE, TOFFEE, SWEET, FLORAL, SOUR, TOASTED, FRUITY, HERBAL

Appearance	Value For Money	Flavor
★☆☆☆☆	★☆☆☆☆	★☆☆☆☆

Would you try again?		Overall Rating
☐ YES	☐ NO	★☆☆☆☆

Cigar Tasting Journal

	NAME				
	BRAND			TYPE	
	WRAPPER			FILLER	
	ORIGIN			SAMPLED	

Label

CIGAR LABEL HERE

Flavor Meter

		VERY MILD	MILD	MEDIUM	MED-FULL	FULL
	BODY					
	FLAVOR					
	STRENGTH					

Notes

Flavor Wheel

Appearance	Value For Money	Flavor
★☆☆☆☆	★☆☆☆☆	★☆☆☆☆

Would you try again?		Overall Rating
☐ YES	☐ NO	★☆☆☆☆

Cigar Tasting Journal

	NAME	
	BRAND	
	WRAPPER	
	ORIGIN	

	TYPE	
	FILLER	
	SAMPLED	

Label

CIGAR LABEL HERE

Flavor Meter

		VERY MILD	MILD	MEDIUM	MED-FULL	FULL
	BODY					
	FLAVOR					
	STRENGTH					

Notes

Flavor Wheel

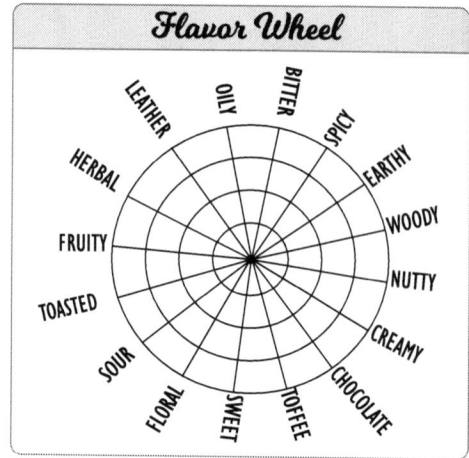

Leather, Oily, Bitter, Spicy, Earthy, Woody, Nutty, Creamy, Chocolate, Toffee, Sweet, Floral, Sour, Toasted, Fruity, Herbal

Appearance	Value For Money	Flavor
★☆☆☆☆	★☆☆☆☆	★☆☆☆☆

Would you try again?		Overall Rating
☐ YES	☐ NO	★☆☆☆☆

Cigar Tasting Journal

NAME			
BRAND		TYPE	
WRAPPER		FILLER	
ORIGIN		SAMPLED	

Label

CIGAR LABEL HERE

Flavor Meter

	VERY MILD	MILD	MEDIUM	MED-FULL	FULL
BODY					
FLAVOR					
STRENGTH					

Notes

Flavor Wheel

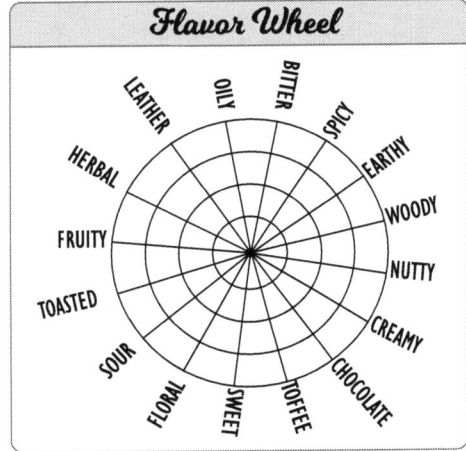

LEATHER · OILY · BITTER · SPICY · EARTHY · WOODY · NUTTY · CREAMY · CHOCOLATE · TOFFEE · SWEET · FLORAL · SOUR · TOASTED · FRUITY · HERBAL

Appearance	Value For Money	Flavor
★☆☆☆☆	★☆☆☆☆	★☆☆☆☆

Would you try again?	Overall Rating
☐ YES ☐ NO	★☆☆☆☆

Cigar Tasting Journal

	NAME			
	BRAND		TYPE	
	WRAPPER		FILLER	
	ORIGIN		SAMPLED	

Label

Flavor Meter

		VERY MILD	MILD	MEDIUM	MED-FULL	FULL
	BODY					
	FLAVOR					
	STRENGTH					

Notes

Flavor Wheel

Appearance	Value For Money	Flavor
★☆☆☆☆	★☆☆☆☆	★☆☆☆☆

Would you try again?	Overall Rating
☐ YES ☐ NO	★☆☆☆☆

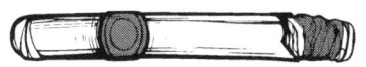

Cigar Tasting Journal

	NAME				
	BRAND			TYPE	
	WRAPPER			FILLER	
	ORIGIN			SAMPLED	

Label

CIGAR LABEL HERE

Flavor Meter

		VERY MILD	MILD	MEDIUM	MED-FULL	FULL
	BODY	VERY MILD	MILD	MEDIUM	MED-FULL	FULL
	FLAVOR	VERY MILD	MILD	MEDIUM	MED-FULL	FULL
	STRENGTH	VERY MILD	MILD	MEDIUM	MED-FULL	FULL

Notes

Flavor Wheel

LEATHER · OILY · BITTER · SPICY · EARTHY · WOODY · NUTTY · CREAMY · CHOCOLATE · TOFFEE · SWEET · FLORAL · SOUR · TOASTED · FRUITY · HERBAL

Appearance	Value For Money	Flavor
★☆☆☆☆	★☆☆☆☆	★☆☆☆☆

Would you try again?		Overall Rating
☐ YES	☐ NO	★☆☆☆☆

Cigar Tasting Journal

NAME			
BRAND		TYPE	
WRAPPER		FILLER	
ORIGIN		SAMPLED	

Label

Flavor Meter

	VERY MILD	MILD	MEDIUM	MED-FULL	FULL
BODY					
FLAVOR					
STRENGTH					

Notes

Flavor Wheel

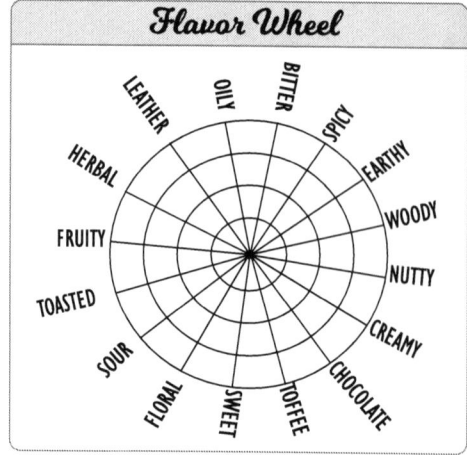

LEATHER · OILY · BITTER · SPICY · EARTHY · WOODY · NUTTY · CREAMY · CHOCOLATE · TOFFEE · SWEET · FLORAL · SOUR · TOASTED · FRUITY · HERBAL

Appearance	Value For Money	Flavor
★☆☆☆☆	★☆☆☆☆	★☆☆☆☆

Would you try again?		Overall Rating
☐ YES	☐ NO	★☆☆☆☆

Cigar Tasting Journal

NAME			
BRAND		TYPE	
WRAPPER		FILLER	
ORIGIN		SAMPLED	

Label

Flavor Meter

	VERY MILD	MILD	MEDIUM	MED-FULL	FULL
BODY					
FLAVOR					
STRENGTH					

Notes

Flavor Wheel

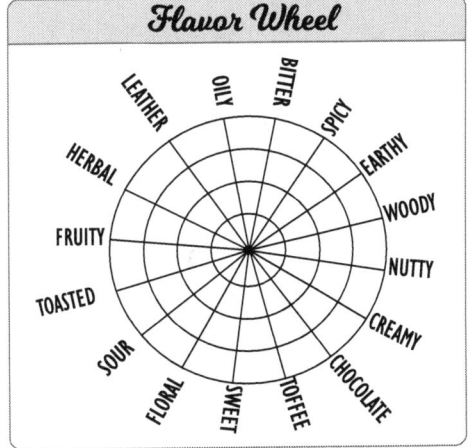

Appearance	Value For Money	Flavor
★☆☆☆☆	★☆☆☆☆	★☆☆☆☆

Would you try again?	Overall Rating
☐ YES ☐ NO	★☆☆☆☆

Cigar Tasting Journal

NAME				
BRAND		TYPE		
WRAPPER		FILLER		
ORIGIN		SAMPLED		

Label

Flavor Meter

	VERY MILD	MILD	MEDIUM	MED-FULL	FULL
BODY					
FLAVOR					
STRENGTH					

Notes

Flavor Wheel

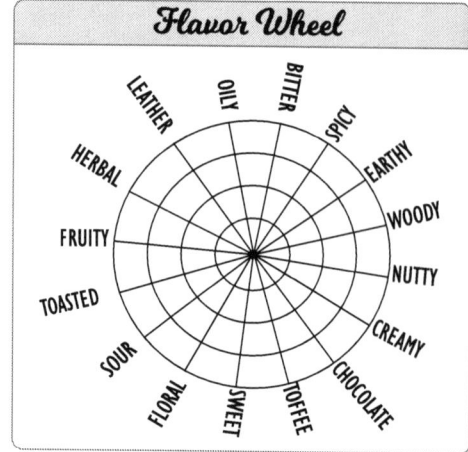

LEATHER, OILY, BITTER, SPICY, EARTHY, WOODY, NUTTY, CREAMY, CHOCOLATE, TOFFEE, SWEET, FLORAL, SOUR, TOASTED, FRUITY, HERBAL

Appearance	Value For Money	Flavor
★☆☆☆☆	★☆☆☆☆	★☆☆☆☆

Would you try again?		Overall Rating
☐ YES	☐ NO	★☆☆☆☆

Cigar Tasting Journal

	NAME				
	BRAND			TYPE	
	WRAPPER			FILLER	
	ORIGIN			SAMPLED	

Label

CIGAR LABEL HERE

Flavor Meter

	BODY	VERY MILD	MILD	MEDIUM	MED-FULL	FULL
	FLAVOR	VERY MILD	MILD	MEDIUM	MED-FULL	FULL
	STRENGTH	VERY MILD	MILD	MEDIUM	MED-FULL	FULL

Notes

Flavor Wheel

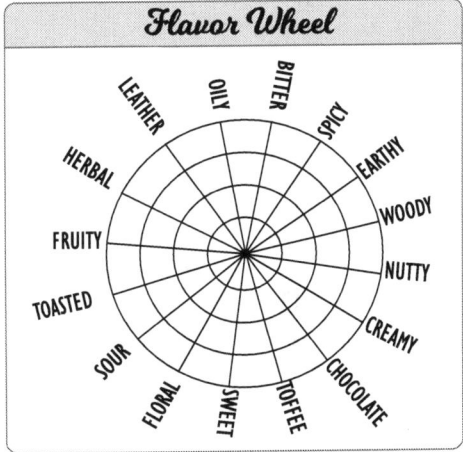

LEATHER, OILY, BITTER, SPICY, EARTHY, WOODY, NUTTY, CREAMY, CHOCOLATE, TOFFEE, SWEET, FLORAL, SOUR, TOASTED, FRUITY, HERBAL

Appearance	Value For Money	Flavor
★☆☆☆☆	★☆☆☆☆	★☆☆☆☆

Would you try again?		Overall Rating
☐ YES	☐ NO	★☆☆☆☆

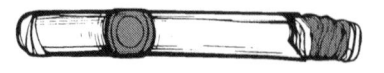

Cigar Tasting Journal

	NAME			TYPE	
	BRAND			FILLER	
	WRAPPER			SAMPLED	
	ORIGIN				

Label

CIGAR LABEL HERE

Flavor Meter

BODY	VERY MILD	MILD	MEDIUM	MED-FULL	FULL
FLAVOR	VERY MILD	MILD	MEDIUM	MED-FULL	FULL
STRENGTH	VERY MILD	MILD	MEDIUM	MED-FULL	FULL

Notes

Flavor Wheel

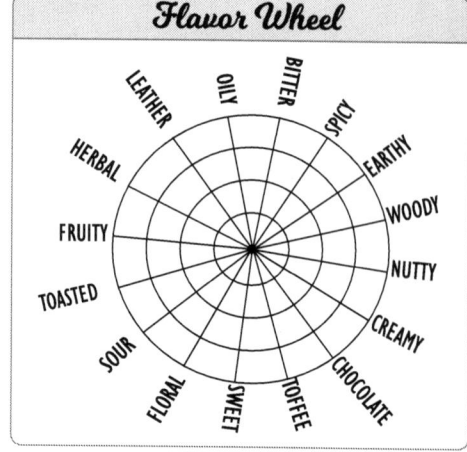

Appearance	Value For Money	Flavor
★☆☆☆☆	★☆☆☆☆	★☆☆☆☆

Would you try again?		Overall Rating
☐ YES	☐ NO	★☆☆☆☆

Cigar Tasting Journal

	NAME				
	BRAND			TYPE	
	WRAPPER			FILLER	
	ORIGIN			SAMPLED	

Label

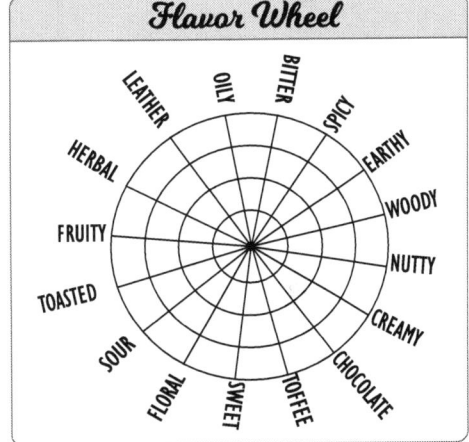

Flavor Meter

	BODY	VERY MILD	MILD	MEDIUM	MED-FULL	FULL
	FLAVOR	VERY MILD	MILD	MEDIUM	MED-FULL	FULL
	STRENGTH	VERY MILD	MILD	MEDIUM	MED-FULL	FULL

Notes

Flavor Wheel

LEATHER, OILY, BITTER, SPICY, EARTHY, WOODY, NUTTY, CREAMY, CHOCOLATE, TOFFEE, SWEET, FLORAL, SOUR, TOASTED, FRUITY, HERBAL

Appearance	Value For Money	Flavor
★☆☆☆☆	★☆☆☆☆	★☆☆☆☆

Would you try again?		Overall Rating
☐ YES	☐ NO	★☆☆☆☆

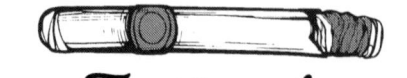

Cigar Tasting Journal

	NAME				
	BRAND			TYPE	
	WRAPPER			FILLER	
	ORIGIN			SAMPLED	

Label

Flavor Meter

		VERY MILD	MILD	MEDIUM	MED-FULL	FULL
	BODY					
	FLAVOR					
	STRENGTH					

Notes

Flavor Wheel

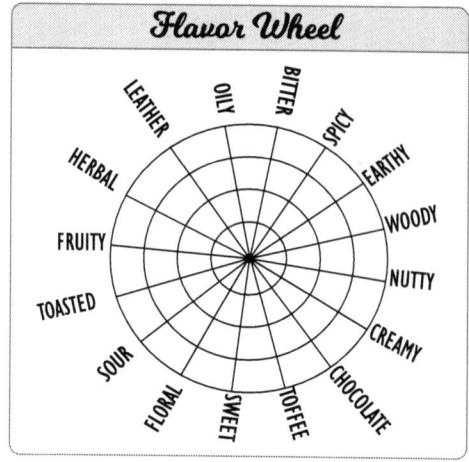

LEATHER, OILY, BITTER, SPICY, EARTHY, WOODY, NUTTY, CREAMY, CHOCOLATE, TOFFEE, SWEET, FLORAL, SOUR, TOASTED, FRUITY, HERBAL

Appearance	Value For Money	Flavor
★☆☆☆☆	★☆☆☆☆	★☆☆☆☆

Would you try again?		Overall Rating
☐ YES	☐ NO	★☆☆☆☆

Cigar Tasting Journal

NAME				
BRAND		TYPE		
WRAPPER		FILLER		
ORIGIN		SAMPLED		

Label

CIGAR LABEL HERE

Flavor Meter

	VERY MILD	MILD	MEDIUM	MED-FULL	FULL
BODY					
FLAVOR					
STRENGTH					

Notes

Flavor Wheel

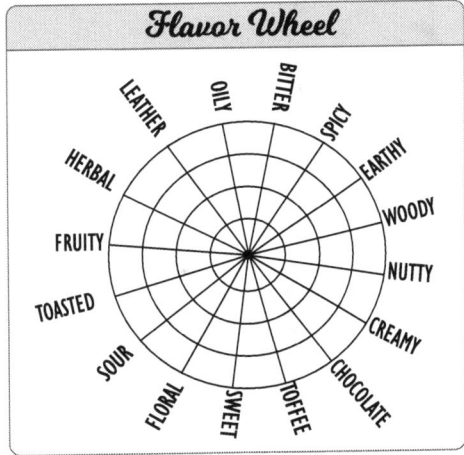

Flavors: BITTER, SPICY, EARTHY, WOODY, NUTTY, CREAMY, CHOCOLATE, TOFFEE, SWEET, FLORAL, SOUR, TOASTED, FRUITY, HERBAL, LEATHER, OILY

Appearance	Value For Money	Flavor
☆☆☆☆☆	☆☆☆☆☆	☆☆☆☆☆

Would you try again?		Overall Rating
☐ YES	☐ NO	☆☆☆☆☆

Cigar Tasting Journal

	NAME				
	BRAND			TYPE	
	WRAPPER			FILLER	
	ORIGIN			SAMPLED	

Label

CIGAR LABEL HERE

Flavor Meter

BODY	VERY MILD	MILD	MEDIUM	MED-FULL	FULL
FLAVOR	VERY MILD	MILD	MEDIUM	MED-FULL	FULL
STRENGTH	VERY MILD	MILD	MEDIUM	MED-FULL	FULL

Notes

Flavor Wheel

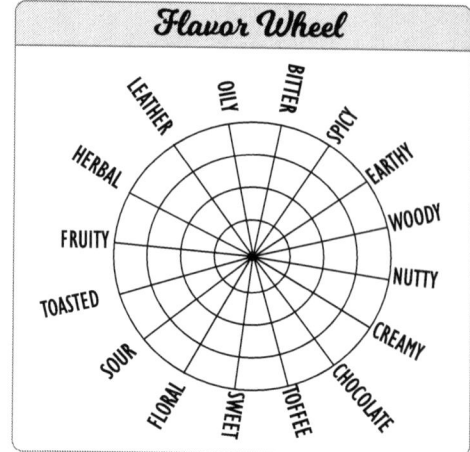

LEATHER · OILY · BITTER · SPICY · EARTHY · WOODY · NUTTY · CREAMY · CHOCOLATE · TOFFEE · SWEET · FLORAL · SOUR · TOASTED · FRUITY · HERBAL

Appearance	Value For Money	Flavor
★☆☆☆☆	★☆☆☆☆	★☆☆☆☆

Would you try again?	Overall Rating
☐ YES ☐ NO	★☆☆☆☆

Cigar Tasting Journal

	NAME				
	BRAND			TYPE	
	WRAPPER			FILLER	
	ORIGIN			SAMPLED	

Label

CIGAR LABEL HERE

Flavor Meter

BODY	VERY MILD	MILD	MEDIUM	MED-FULL	FULL
FLAVOR	VERY MILD	MILD	MEDIUM	MED-FULL	FULL
STRENGTH	VERY MILD	MILD	MEDIUM	MED-FULL	FULL

Notes

Flavor Wheel

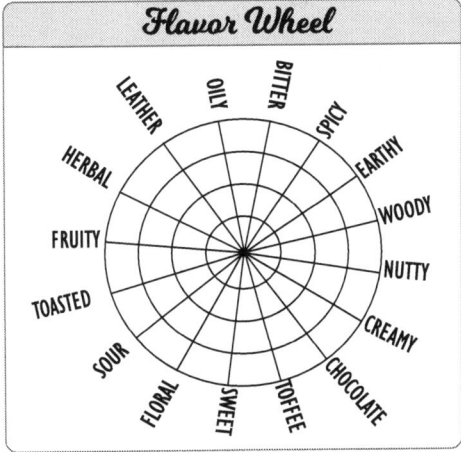

BITTER, OILY, LEATHER, SPICY, EARTHY, HERBAL, WOODY, FRUITY, NUTTY, TOASTED, CREAMY, SOUR, CHOCOLATE, FLORAL, SWEET, TOFFEE

Appearance	Value For Money	Flavor
★☆☆☆☆	★☆☆☆☆	★☆☆☆☆

Would you try again?	Overall Rating
☐ YES ☐ NO	★☆☆☆☆

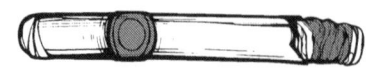

Cigar Tasting Journal

NAME		TYPE	
BRAND		FILLER	
WRAPPER		SAMPLED	
ORIGIN			

Label

CIGAR LABEL HERE

Flavor Meter

	VERY MILD	MILD	MEDIUM	MED-FULL	FULL
BODY					
FLAVOR					
STRENGTH					

Notes

Flavor Wheel

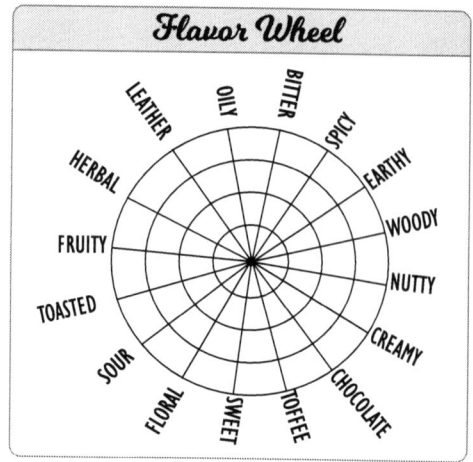

Appearance	Value For Money	Flavor
⭐☆☆☆☆	⭐☆☆☆☆	⭐☆☆☆☆

Would you try again?	Overall Rating
☐ YES ☐ NO	⭐☆☆☆☆

Cigar Tasting Journal

NAME				
BRAND		TYPE		
WRAPPER		FILLER		
ORIGIN		SAMPLED		

Label

CIGAR LABEL HERE

Flavor Meter

	VERY MILD	MILD	MEDIUM	MED-FULL	FULL
BODY					
FLAVOR					
STRENGTH					

Notes

Flavor Wheel

LEATHER, OILY, BITTER, SPICY, EARTHY, WOODY, NUTTY, CREAMY, CHOCOLATE, TOFFEE, SWEET, FLORAL, SOUR, TOASTED, FRUITY, HERBAL

Appearance	Value For Money	Flavor
★☆☆☆☆	★☆☆☆☆	★☆☆☆☆

Would you try again?	Overall Rating
☐ YES ☐ NO	★☆☆☆☆

Cigar Tasting Journal

	NAME	
	BRAND	
	WRAPPER	
	ORIGIN	

	TYPE	
	FILLER	
	SAMPLED	

Label

CIGAR LABEL HERE

Flavor Meter

		VERY MILD	MILD	MEDIUM	MED-FULL	FULL
	BODY					
	FLAVOR					
	STRENGTH					

Notes

Flavor Wheel

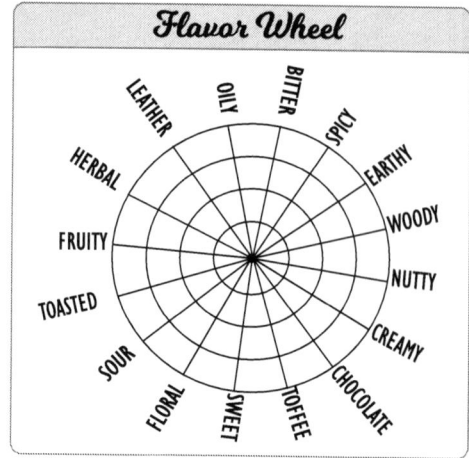

LEATHER · OILY · BITTER · SPICY · EARTHY · WOODY · NUTTY · CREAMY · CHOCOLATE · TOFFEE · SWEET · FLORAL · SOUR · TOASTED · FRUITY · HERBAL

Appearance	Value For Money	Flavor
★☆☆☆☆	★☆☆☆☆	★☆☆☆☆

Would you try again?	Overall Rating
☐ YES ☐ NO	★☆☆☆☆

Cigar Tasting Journal

NAME			
BRAND		TYPE	
WRAPPER		FILLER	
ORIGIN		SAMPLED	

Label

CIGAR LABEL HERE

Flavor Meter

	VERY MILD	MILD	MEDIUM	MED-FULL	FULL
BODY					
FLAVOR					
STRENGTH					

Notes

Flavor Wheel

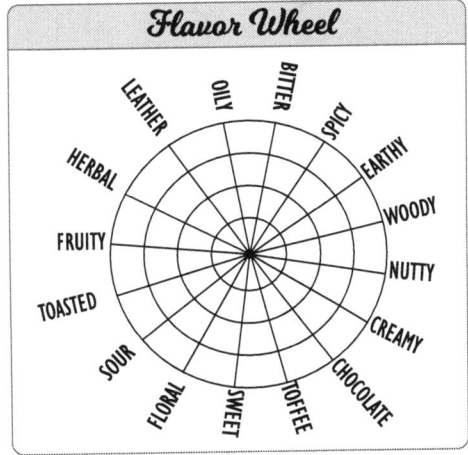

Appearance	Value For Money	Flavor
⭐☆☆☆☆	⭐☆☆☆☆	⭐☆☆☆☆

Would you try again?		Overall Rating
☐ YES	☐ NO	⭐☆☆☆☆

Cigar Tasting Journal

	NAME				
	BRAND			TYPE	
	WRAPPER			FILLER	
	ORIGIN			SAMPLED	

Label

CIGAR LABEL HERE

Flavor Meter

		VERY MILD	MILD	MEDIUM	MED-FULL	FULL
	BODY					
	FLAVOR					
	STRENGTH					

Notes

Flavor Wheel

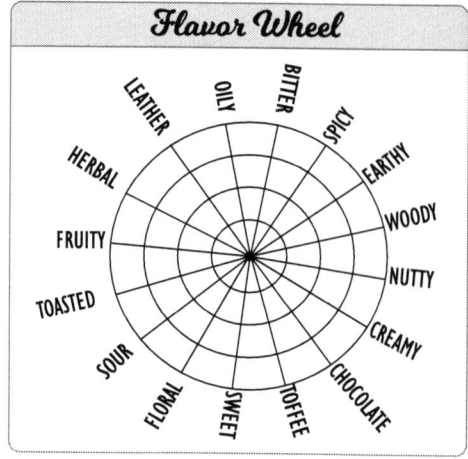

Appearance	Value For Money	Flavor
★☆☆☆☆	★☆☆☆☆	★☆☆☆☆

Would you try again?		Overall Rating
☐ YES	☐ NO	★☆☆☆☆

Cigar Tasting Journal

NAME			
BRAND		TYPE	
WRAPPER		FILLER	
ORIGIN		SAMPLED	

Label

CIGAR LABEL HERE

Flavor Meter

	VERY MILD	MILD	MEDIUM	MED-FULL	FULL
BODY					
FLAVOR					
STRENGTH					

Notes

Flavor Wheel

LEATHER, OILY, BITTER, SPICY, EARTHY, WOODY, NUTTY, CREAMY, CHOCOLATE, TOFFEE, SWEET, FLORAL, SOUR, TOASTED, FRUITY, HERBAL

Appearance	Value For Money	Flavor
★☆☆☆☆	★☆☆☆☆	★☆☆☆☆

Would you try again?	Overall Rating
☐ YES ☐ NO	★☆☆☆☆

Cigar Tasting Journal

	NAME				
	BRAND			TYPE	
	WRAPPER			FILLER	
	ORIGIN			SAMPLED	

Label

CIGAR LABEL HERE

Flavor Meter

	BODY	VERY MILD	MILD	MEDIUM	MED-FULL	FULL
	FLAVOR	VERY MILD	MILD	MEDIUM	MED-FULL	FULL
	STRENGTH	VERY MILD	MILD	MEDIUM	MED-FULL	FULL

Notes

Flavor Wheel

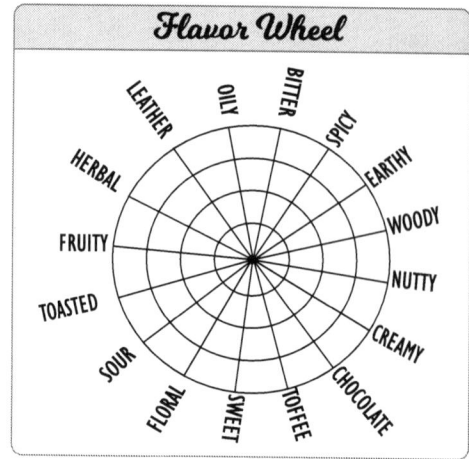

LEATHER · OILY · BITTER · SPICY · EARTHY · WOODY · NUTTY · CREAMY · CHOCOLATE · TOFFEE · SWEET · FLORAL · SOUR · TOASTED · FRUITY · HERBAL

Appearance	Value For Money	Flavor
★☆☆☆☆	★☆☆☆☆	★☆☆☆☆

Would you try again?	Overall Rating
☐ YES ☐ NO	★☆☆☆☆

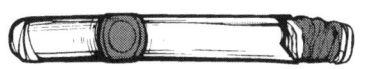

Cigar Tasting Journal

	NAME				
	BRAND			TYPE	
	WRAPPER			FILLER	
	ORIGIN			SAMPLED	

Label

CIGAR LABEL HERE

Flavor Meter

		VERY MILD	MILD	MEDIUM	MED-FULL	FULL
	BODY					
	FLAVOR					
	STRENGTH					

Notes

Flavor Wheel

Appearance	Value For Money	Flavor
⭐☆☆☆☆	⭐☆☆☆☆	⭐☆☆☆☆

Would you try again?		Overall Rating
☐ YES	☐ NO	⭐☆☆☆☆

Cigar Tasting Journal

	NAME				
	BRAND			TYPE	
	WRAPPER			FILLER	
	ORIGIN			SAMPLED	

Label

CIGAR LABEL HERE

Flavor Meter

		VERY MILD	MILD	MEDIUM	MED-FULL	FULL
	BODY					
	FLAVOR					
	STRENGTH					

Notes

Flavor Wheel

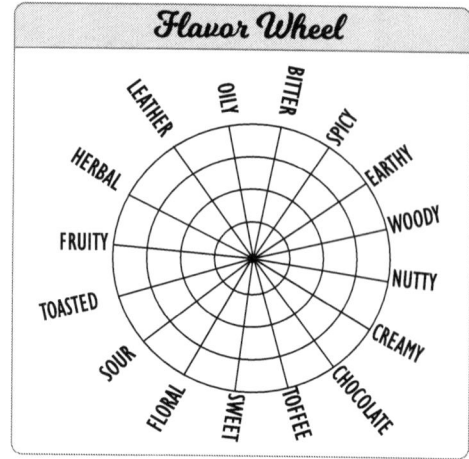

LEATHER · OILY · BITTER · SPICY · EARTHY · WOODY · NUTTY · CREAMY · CHOCOLATE · TOFFEE · SWEET · FLORAL · SOUR · TOASTED · FRUITY · HERBAL

Appearance	Value For Money	Flavor
★☆☆☆☆	★☆☆☆☆	★☆☆☆☆

Would you try again?		Overall Rating
☐ YES	☐ NO	★☆☆☆☆

Cigar Tasting Journal

NAME			
BRAND		TYPE	
WRAPPER		FILLER	
ORIGIN		SAMPLED	

Label

CIGAR LABEL HERE

Flavor Meter

	VERY MILD	MILD	MEDIUM	MED-FULL	FULL
BODY					
FLAVOR					
STRENGTH					

Notes

Flavor Wheel

LEATHER · OILY · BITTER · SPICY · EARTHY · WOODY · NUTTY · CREAMY · CHOCOLATE · TOFFEE · SWEET · FLORAL · SOUR · TOASTED · FRUITY · HERBAL

Appearance	Value For Money	Flavor
★☆☆☆☆	★☆☆☆☆	★☆☆☆☆

Would you try again?	Overall Rating
☐ YES ☐ NO	★☆☆☆☆

Cigar Tasting Journal

	NAME			
	BRAND		TYPE	
	WRAPPER		FILLER	
	ORIGIN		SAMPLED	

Label

CIGAR LABEL HERE

Flavor Meter

		VERY MILD	MILD	MEDIUM	MED-FULL	FULL
	BODY					
	FLAVOR					
	STRENGTH					

Notes

Flavor Wheel

LEATHER · OILY · BITTER · SPICY · EARTHY · WOODY · NUTTY · CREAMY · CHOCOLATE · TOFFEE · SWEET · FLORAL · SOUR · TOASTED · FRUITY · HERBAL

Appearance	Value For Money	Flavor
★☆☆☆☆	★☆☆☆☆	★☆☆☆☆

Would you try again?	Overall Rating
☐ YES ☐ NO	★☆☆☆☆

Cigar Tasting Journal

NAME				
BRAND		TYPE		
WRAPPER		FILLER		
ORIGIN		SAMPLED		

Label

CIGAR LABEL HERE

Flavor Meter

	VERY MILD	MILD	MEDIUM	MED-FULL	FULL
BODY					
FLAVOR					
STRENGTH					

Notes

Flavor Wheel

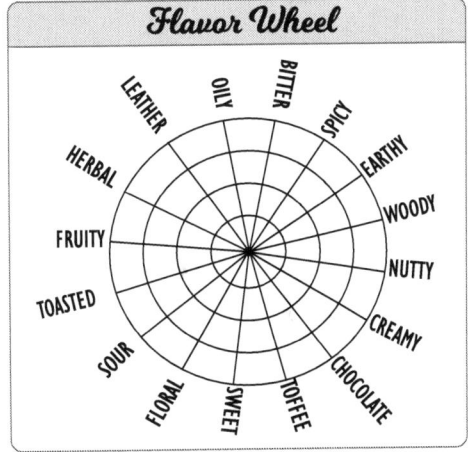

Appearance	Value For Money	Flavor
★☆☆☆☆	★☆☆☆☆	★☆☆☆☆

Would you try again?	Overall Rating
☐ YES ☐ NO	★☆☆☆☆

Cigar Tasting Journal

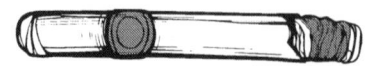

	NAME				
	BRAND			TYPE	
	WRAPPER			FILLER	
	ORIGIN			SAMPLED	

Label

CIGAR LABEL HERE

Flavor Meter

BODY	VERY MILD	MILD	MEDIUM	MED-FULL	FULL
FLAVOR	VERY MILD	MILD	MEDIUM	MED-FULL	FULL
STRENGTH	VERY MILD	MILD	MEDIUM	MED-FULL	FULL

Notes

Flavor Wheel

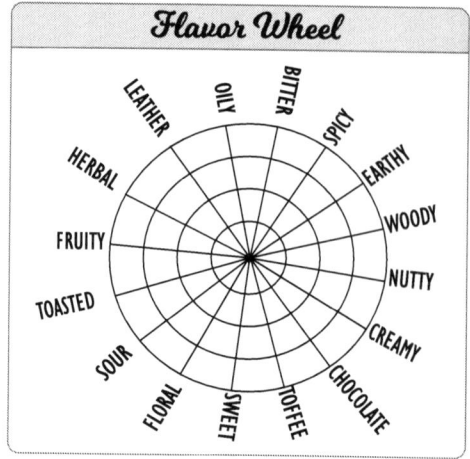

Appearance	Value For Money	Flavor
★☆☆☆☆	★☆☆☆☆	★☆☆☆☆

Would you try again?		Overall Rating
☐ YES	☐ NO	★☆☆☆☆

Made in the USA
Middletown, DE
20 March 2024